Broke, Broken

What College Doesn't Teach You About Money

By Pedro M. Frias

"Stop talking yourself out of opportunities because you feel like you're not ready yet. It's time to jump. You are ready now!"

Pedro M. Frias
via Instagram

Contents

Contents

About the Author

Pedro M. Frias is the founder and CEO of Blacklyst and a former financial adviser for both Merrill Lynch and Morgan Stanley in Boston. After flunking out of college multiple times before age twenty, he defaulted on over $20,000 in student loan debt and was sued by the US government.

Faced with the reality of that difficult situation, he did not fold. Even when everyone seemed to doubt him, he determined to finance his own education, made a series of other tough decisions, and started slowly turning his life around.

Originally from Worcester, MA, Frias is the son of blue-collar, Dominican-American parents who immigrated here with the hopes of realizing the American Dream.

After going back to college at Nichols more dedicated than ever, he later graduated cum laude with a degree in Finance.

Frias is fluent in both English and Spanish, has amassed thousands of online followers in recent years, and is a former licensed wealth manager (with a series 7 and 66) for Morgan Stanley and Merrill Lynch.

He has taken key roles at tech companies like Google before founding his own firm, and he's had the privilege of planning events for numerous high-profile non-profits, athletes, and celebrities.

He fights every day to support those from a similar background who often find themselves in the challenging position of having to bounce back—often without the same wealth management tools the wealthy enjoy.

For the first time, he has put all that information into one, easily digestible format, and he has dedicated it to anyone feeling broke and broken (as he once did). It is his sincerest hope it will uplift your spirits—and send you into the new year more prepared than ever!

Chapter 1

Broke, Broken

OVERVIEW

In 2008, the United States was on the brink of a total financial meltdown, the likes of which had not been seen in decades. It would later be dubbed the "Great Recession."

Housing prices plummeted. There was a massive liquidity crisis. Americans watched as their 401k's, Roth IRA's, real estate, and other personal assets and investments imploded.

There was panic in the streets—from Wall Street to Main Street to all points in between.

Not surprisingly, academia kept right on moving completely undeterred because they more or less operate in a vacuum, utterly oblivious to the realities of the outside world. Plus, what they do not teach you is every bit as important as what they do, as the whole landscape is continuously shifting in terms of what's new and essential.

In terms of the '08 crash, it was the perfect financial storm. In hindsight, we were collectively forced to confront a bunch of tough lessons, and I'd like to say things are finally moving in the right direction.

Since that time, the stock market has soared, real estate has rebounded, unemployment rates are low, and real GDP growth has stayed comparatively high quarter by quarter and year by year (albeit distorted by deficit spending).

With a quick glance of any Wall Street ticker, you might say it's smooth sailing now. But it depends on who you ask.

Are we on the verge of another bear market—or a recession—as some experts predict?

There is no doubt we're not out of the weeds, and the likelihood of another economic downturn in the next couple of years (or sooner) is increasingly more likely. In fact, it's just the nature of the markets and capitalism.

But its also one more reason to invest in yourself and what you know—if you haven't already.

Of course, if you're one of the 1%, you don't have much to worry about nowadays, except what kind of sweetener you prefer in your favorite latte or which color you want for your new Range Rover.

Which one do you prefer? Splenda? Sugar?

The chances are you're not a member of the 1%, no matter what preferred sweetener you choose. If you are, you have a bevy of attorneys, financial analysts, business associates, and more information than you can reasonably process (without their help), all to make you more money and use the money you already have for more significant gains.

On the flip side, if you're a member of the other 99%, life looks a little bit different than it does for the average Fortune 500 exec or pro sports team owner.

You may be wrestling with student loan debt, mountainous credit card and other personal debt, hyperinflating health care and education costs, and stagnant wages—to name a few of the most pressing issues confronting the middle-class today.

Moreover, one of the cornerstones of achieving the American Dream, homeownership, is an increasingly unrealistic option for you, not to mention, there's a genuine debate between owning versus renting in the first place.

Neither of those options will work for you if you're wrestling with one or more of the aforementioned issues, still living at home, and having little optimism for the upcoming years. In short, you may be feeling broke and broken.

So, when we say middle-class, what exactly do we mean by that? In this country in the year 2020, what does it mean, and has it always meant the same thing?

We'll get into more of the numbers, but being a member of the middle-class generally means you work for a living (whether by the hour or designated salary). You sell the best hours of your day to someone who typically focuses on earning profits.

For that matter, life is entirely less comfortable for you if you're in the middle-class versus upper-class, and there are many other differences, too.

The middle-class tends to spend money and buy "stuff," while the wealthy tend to use their money to make more money. The middle-class seem wholly unable to save money, while the wealthy are far savvier than the poor or middle-class.

There are numerous other stunning differences between the wealthy and the middle-class, but let's look at the data.

Using the latest numbers available, the average salary of someone who's 16-20 comes to about $23,322 per year according to the Bureau of Labor Statistics (BLS), which comes to about $448.50 per week.[a]

From the same source, the average salary of someone who's 20-24, comes to about $29,770 or only about $572.50 per week; and the average salary of someone who's 25-34 comes to about $41,951 or about $806.75 per week, which is where we notice a discernable increase over previous years.

If we keep going, the average salary for someone who's 35-44 comes to about $51,272 or about $986 per week, another increase over previous years.

However, the average salary of someone who's 45-54 is about $52,143 or about $1,002.75, another hike, albeit slightly less notable; finally, those income increases abruptly drop-off as we move into the 65 and older range, as you may imagine.

We can break it down even further in terms of the wage gap denoted in the following chart.[b]

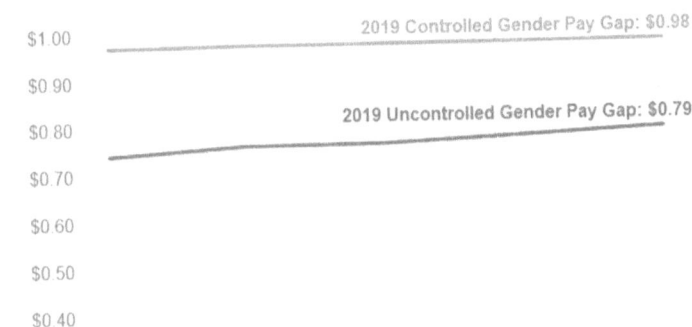

The Gender Pay Gap Over Time
Using PayScale's crowdsourced compensation data

As you can see, if you're a woman or minority, there's a significant drop-off in earnings—across the board, on average, in this country.

It's 2020, for example, and women are still only earning about 79-cents per every dollar men do—and that amount only varies slightly per whatever study you reference.[c]

If you look at Latinas, the wage gap is even more startling. For example, Latinas only earn about 54-cents on the dollar to their white male counterparts in this country—keeping in mind, that's for doing the exact same job per our research.[d]

In the next chart, "uncontrolled" versus "controlled" refers to whether or not the respondents had a degree. We can reasonably infer whether you are degreed (or not) that the wage gap is very real despite certain dialogue to the contrary.[e]

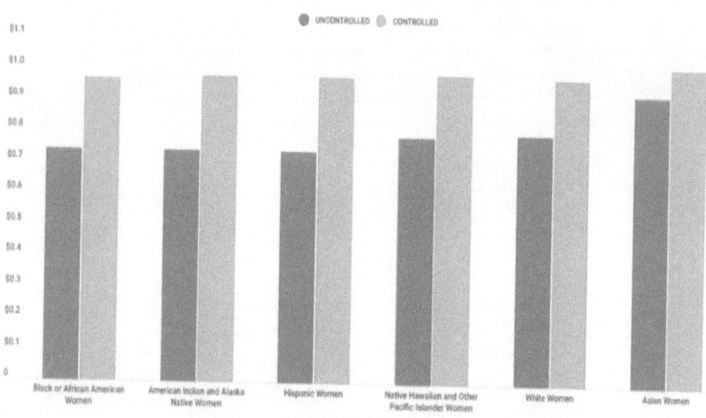

As the data indicates, how much money you can reasonably expect to earn is directly related to your gender and ethnicity; however, we will not be disputing that in this text, as, admittedly, it's outside our purview.

Our primary purpose is to confront the realities of the middle-class as we seek to empower our readers with many of the tools they can use to create and/or maintain their wealth.

What makes this infinitely more complicated is that there are additional challenges facing the middle-class, particularly concerning millennials.

For starters, the student loan fiasco is at a boiling point, as more and more Americans are finding themselves with mountainous unpaid debt hanging over them like a dark cloud, dampening what might otherwise be a far brighter future.

As of 2019, according to Forbes, there are nearly 45 million borrowers who collectively owe more than $1.5 trillion in student loan debt in the United States, making student loan debt the second-highest category of consumer debt behind only mortgage debt and higher than both credit cards and auto loans.[f]

From the same source (using numbers per the Institute for College Access and Success), borrowers in the class of 2017, on average, owed $28,650.

Furthermore, from that source, student loan delinquency or defaults are reaching all-time highs at over 11.4%, accounting for $101.4 billion cumulative defaults representing more than 5.1 million borrowers.

That's over five million Americans who are feeling broke and broken, who are no doubt debating on whether to pay their student loan debt or have a place to lay their heads or food to eat.

On the other hand, there are many Americans who do not have to worry about student loan debt and similar related issues by virtue of birthright.

Those same people have access to fancy Wall Street wealth managers, insider deals, innumerable unique opportunities, and privileged information.

Before the JOBS Act of 2009, which was passed by then-President Barrack Obama, you had to be an actual "accredited investor" to invest in pre-public startups, a little-known fact that still alludes many Americans.

What the JOBS Act did was opened up equity and product crowdfunding to the general public, although many of the outdated laws were mostly if not entirely unaffected.

Buying traditional securities from pre-public startups is still based on pre-JOBS Act, SEC guidelines dating back to the 1920s, and what that means is if you wanted to invest in Facebook or Uber, for example, you were not allowed to unless you were an "accredited investor."

A hypothetical $10,000 investment in Facebook before "The Facebook" became "Facebook," as we know it, would have netted you millions in returns later, but per the above-mentioned guidelines, it was not and is not permissible.

However, our hope is that equity crowdfunding will slowly start to supplant Angels and VC's as the most common means of startup fundraising in the coming years.

An **ACCREDITED INVESTOR** (words in ALL CAPS and BOLD are in our appendix for further info) is someone who, by law, can prove they earn over $250,000 per year for the previous two years and have a net wealth of over $2.5 million (excluding their primary place of residence) in case you were wondering.

Ergo, the term "accredited investor" can simply be interchanged with the more familiar term, "millionaire," for the most part, and we all know what a millionaire is.

THE OTHER 99%

Those same SEC guidelines still exist today, although, through the advent of equity and product crowdfunding, there are now new opportunities for average Americans to invest in startups, buy actual equity, and potentially earn handsome returns.

It's a high-risk, high-reward endeavor, but if part of a larger, more comprehensive investment strategy, it could make sense for you (Kickstarter and Indiegogo are two such platforms you could use to potentially get started).

We've established that you're most likely not an accredited investor—or "wealthy." There are many other differences between the rich and the middle-class, but this book isn't about the 1%, and it is not some off-handed attempt to demonize the wealthy or whites, for that matter.

This book is about the other 99%, and more importantly, it is about empowering you to improve your life by taking advantage of many of the same great techniques your wealthier counterparts have been utilizing for years.

To those ends, we will explore and explode entrenched ideas, inefficiencies, and biases inherent to the traditional system of wealth creation and money management in this country, while helping readers understand and successfully navigate the all-too-tricky world of finance, the macro-economy, personal investing, and money management.

We've incorporated a fictional character, Claudia, whose parents immigrated into this country from Guadalajara, Mexico, in recent years. Claudia is looking to make better financial decisions in her life moving forward, plan for college, open a business, and in the immediate future, move out of her parent's house.

Claudia is you! She feels broke and broken. In some ways, she may even look and act like you or someone you know.

However, I assure you, that's completely coincidental, as she is entirely the figment of my imagination and only used to help guide you through the process as if you were walking into a financial manager's office yourself.

Before meeting our fictional friend, let's take a brief look at the following key pillars of our approach before proceeding. We will be covering each one of these critical concepts in more detail in subsequent chapters.

THE KEY PILLARS OF BROKE, BROKEN

1. There are numerous startling differences between the wealthy and the middle-class in the US. The idea is not to demonize the wealthy. The idea is to increase the amount of information available to average Americans (millennials, middle-class, minorities, etc.), so that they can make informed decisions that will no doubt improve their lives.

2. The middle-class tend to live above their means, while the wealthy tend to live below their means, which is a testament to how the latter group's wealth is created and maintained. Not surprisingly, personal debt is up. Student loan debt is up, and we include several reliable money management techniques to address this glaring issue plaguing millennials and the middle-class.

3. The middle-class have "stuff," while the rich have money and access to creating more of it. They use

their money, leverage it, and earn more of it. Subsequently, wealth (or the lack of it) is a generational issue. We want to explode generational effects of poverty and the whole mindset of scarcity and re-program how people think about money (i.e., how to make it, how to spend it wisely, how to make every dollar count, how to save it, how to invest it, and how to make more of it).

4. The middle-class tends to be emotional in how they deal with money, while the wealthy are far savvier. Of course, this is easier said than done as the middle-class earn far less money than their wealthier counterparts, and that's even further exacerbated if you're a woman or minority, as reflected in the above-listed data. Latinas are hit the hardest with the wage gap, and they face an even steeper climb. However, it's not insurmountable, and we hope this will help.

5. The middle-class often underestimate their potential, while the wealthy have much higher expectations and clear-cut goals. As such, we understand that psychology comes into play in the whole way different groups of people look at money, and we will be discussing some of those psychological implications along with a case study that denotes the astounding ways rich people versus poor people respond when given the same opportunity.

6. The middle-class believe in hard work, while the wealthy believe in earning money; neither one is per se wrong, but only one of these groups genuinely understands how to create long-term wealth.

7. The middle-class tends to be less astute when it comes to market terminology and concepts, while the wealthy tend to be far more knowledgeable about how those concepts work—and ultimately, how to wield those things to their benefit.

8. There is a "hidden economy" in this country, an economy that lurks just below the surface and includes data such as high credit card balances, mountainous student loan debt, wage stagnation, and more. We often get blinded by years of GDP growth and historically low unemployment—and forget to dig deeper, exposing the damaging effects of scarcity and poverty.

9. While this is a sobering portrait of the realities of the middle-class, there is a proverbial pot of gold at the end of the rainbow. You may have to work ten times harder to succeed, but I believe in you, and you can succeed.

10. Financial technology (Fintech) is helping level the playing field and democratize finances for people in each category. My readers need to be aware of these innovations since they are low cost, transparent, have minimum fees, and low barriers.

REVIEW & REFLECT

We will navigate the following chapters with the above-listed pillars in mind, as they represent the general mode of thinking for this inquiry.

I've put important terms and concepts in bolded, all caps, and you can follow-up with those concepts in our glossary in the appendix.

The purpose of "Broke, Broken," is to put the same tools of wealth creation and money management the wealthy enjoy into the hands of regular, blue collar Americans (from a mixture of backgrounds) and help kick-off the slow democratization of the entire way wealth is created and maintained in this country, while completely transforming the way we think about money in the first place. To those ends—and without further ado, let's dive right in!

Chapter 2
Meeting Claudia

INTRODUCTION

"My mom, dad, siblings, and I immigrated to America almost ten years ago, and it was not exactly like I expected," Claudia admitted in nearly perfect, albeit heavily accented-English.

She was a young Latina with long, black, flowing hair, a smile that lit the entire room, and a magnetism that's completely indescribable. A hairdresser by trade, she had recently received her first raise since starting at the salon almost a year ago.

She was now earning about $30,000 per year and felt pretty good about that—but had visions of moving away from home, completing her degree with very little debt, and launching her own chain of salons in the coming years.

For her and her parents, that's what America represented, very the realistic possibility of vertical mobility and the real implications those possibilities spell-out for her and her siblings.

A few minutes earlier, she had walked into the financial advisor's office with a slew of pre-planned questions, namely what and how she could start saving money, as well as some of the basics.

From what she understood, most people do not save (if at all) until much later in life, and she was hoping to not make the same mistakes her parents and others like them made.

A middle-aged man with white tufts of hair greeted her at the door, shook her hand, and asked her to come into his office. Secretly, Claudia chuckled to herself at his wild, unruly eyebrows and hair. But his rosy cheeks and bright smile were warm and welcoming.

Both parties were cordial, and after the initial helloes, she finally said, "I am the oldest of all my siblings, so I have always been a natural leader. I have to set the example for my younger brothers and sisters, explain to them the dangers of the world, share my plans for the future, and hope they follow in my footsteps."

"That's very admirable of you," Carson, our fictional financial advisor, said. "Please tell me more."

"I was at home when we found out my grandfather had been killed. It was a tragic day for my family."

"I'm so sorry for your loss."

"Well, it's actually been almost a decade now, but it still hurts," she recalled. "We are from Guadalajara, Mexico, and it was always my grandparent's dream for all of us to move to America. He knew it would be safer here, and America would afford us the kinds of opportunities they never got to have when they were coming up in and around Guadalajara."

"I understand. And since you've been here, how have things been?" Carson asked, quickly enraptured with her story.

"It's mostly been ok, but I never knew how hard it would be to make it in this country," she admitted. "I thought everyone in America was rich, but as it turns out, everything is so expensive, and it's so just hard to simply keep up."

Carson chuckled, adding, "Well, as you can see, most Americans certainly are not rich. But I'm glad you came to see me today. In fact, you have a riveting story—and I'd like to learn more."

"Thank you," she quipped. "We started at a public school after settling into a nice, little community in the San Diego-area. My grades were always good. My mom works as a waitress. My father works in construction and makes a decent income but in cash."

She continued, "Neither of them completed school. My grandparents could not afford to take care of the family on his income—and my father started working in agriculture from an early age. He later developed some skills with carpentry that he utilizes nowadays. My mother's story was pretty much the same actually. You know, they've had a tough life, but I respect my parents more than anyone else in the world because they've modeled for me what it looks like to be good, honest, hardworking people."

"I think I would like to meet your parents, Claudia," Carson injected. "They seem like good people."

"I think that would be nice. But they aren't nearly as concerned with financial planning as I am, I fear. To be completely honest," she added. "That is exactly why I'm here today. My parents are great people, but they've never been able to save for retirement. I don't think they make enough to save much of anything, truthfully, and that scares me. They can't work forever," she relented.

"That's exactly right," Carson said. "Well, I'm glad you came in today, and it seems to me that you're lightyears ahead of most people your age when it comes to acknowledging how important financial planning can be and just walking through that door over there," he added, pointing. "Was the first step in the right direction."

Claudia nodded and then returned her attention to Carson, seated across his cluttered desk.

"I don't want to look up twenty or thirty years from now with regrets," Claudia said. "I want to do something about that right now. I have big dreams for myself—and my siblings. I want to help my parents retire. I want to graduate college with very little, if any, debt. I want my siblings to have a better life than I had. I want to open up a whole chain of salons one day," she added, her large brown eyes glowing.

"Let me ask you this," Carson replied. "How much do you know about investing, budgeting, or even the macro-economy, in general?"

"Sadly, not a whole lot," Claudia admitted.

"Let's start there and see what we can do for you. I'd like to go over a few basic concepts with you, and then later, we'll get more specific as we move along. Is that okay?" he added, gently repositioning a picture of what looked like a younger version of himself and a beautiful young lady on his desk.

"Thanks! That would be great!" she exclaimed. "I'm pressed for time today, unfortunately. But I do have a few minutes."

"Perfect," Carson replied, briefly pausing as if to gather his thoughts.

He continued, "Let's start with the stock market, securities, stocks, bonds. That sort of thing. How much do you know about the stock market, Miss Claudia?"

She chuckled at his calling her "Miss" and added, "Not much. Oh, and you can just call me Claudia."

"Ok, Claudia, that will be a great place to start then." Carson leaned over from his desk and focused on Claudia more intently.

He had her rapt attention, as he launched into various foundational concepts concerning the economy and investing, knowing they would be able to build on those concepts later.

Let's briefly cover some of the highlights from their first meeting.

OVERVIEW OF THE STOCK MARKET

The stock market is a collection of markets and exchanges where regular, coordinated activities of buying and selling shares of publicly-held companies take place.

When we think stock market, we think tickers, the floor of the NYSE, and maybe even a large statue of a bull on Wall Street at the base of Broadway (the statue is reportedly being moved as of the writing of this book, according to Market Insiders).[g]

Anyone can purchase publicly traded securities within stock exchanges, which are the individual framework of the overall stock market.

The stock market and stock exchange are often interchangeable words, but there are some differences between the two, namely a stock exchange is one piece of the entire stock market's make-up, and the term stock exchange generally denotes a specific place where stocks are bought and sold such as the **NASDAQ** or New York Stock Exchange (**NYSE**), two of the largest stock exchanges in the US.

The stock market is called an equity market because those stocks represent a piece of a company's equity (i.e., ownership), which may be called "securities."

Simply put, when you purchase a stock, you are purchasing equity in a specific company, unless it's a fund, which is a collection of stocks from various companies.

As always, please refer to our glossary in the appendix for further elaboration on many of the terms denoted herein.

There are designated markets for almost every type of commodity, which serve as platforms for where numerous buyers and sellers meet, interact, and transact.

The fact there are so many participants in these transactions has an advantage, namely that buyers tend to be assured of a common, agreed upon price that is considered fair.

A stock market is a designated market for trading various types of securities in a controlled, secured, heavily regulated environment (the Securities and Exchange Commission or SEC oversees various functions of our markets).

A long time ago, stock markets dealt with paper-based share certificates, although in today's age and with the advent of modern computing and other technology, stock markets operate purely electronically.

This is the biggest reason why if you look at the floor of the New York Stock Exchange, for example, there are far fewer people than there used to be, even though the number of transactions has soared over time.

People can transact on the NYSE from all over the world and communicate with one another completely electronically via the internet and a system of highly secured computers and mainframes.

The index that most likely comes to mind when you think about the "stock market" is the **DOW** (which is most commonly used to denote the "Dow Jones Industrial Average," although there are multiple versions of the Dow).

The main Dow is an index that tracks 30 of the largest, publicly owned companies trading on both the NYSE and the NASDAQ. There are various means by which investors and others track the overall health of the economy.

Analyzing the Dow has been commonly used as one part of that equation. When we think about the financial health of an economy, we tend to think about market performance, GDP, debt, and a handful of other major metrics.

In the following chart from Money Morning, we see the top ten largest drops in the history of the Dow and are quickly reminded of the Great Recession of 2008 referenced earlier.[h]

Dow Jones Industrial Average: Top 10 Largest Daily Percentage Losses

MONEY MORNING
YOUR EASY MAP TO FINANCIAL FREEDOM

Rank	Date	Close	Net Change	% Change
1	10-19-1987	1,738.74	-508.00	-22.61
2	10-28-1929	260.64	-38.33	-12.82
3	10-29-1929	230.07	-30.57	-11.73
4	11-06-1929	232.13	-25.55	-9.92
5	12-18-1899	58.27	-5.57	-8.72
6	08-12-1932	63.11	-5.79	-8.40
7	03-14-1907	76.23	-6.89	-8.29
8	10-26-1987	1,793.93	-156.83	-8.04
9	10-15-2008	8,577.91	-733.08	-7.87
10	07-21-1933	88.71	-7.55	-7.84

Source: Wikipedia.org, Money Morning staff research

If we look at net change, the numbers would have looked much different with 5 of the top 10 hardest hit days occurring in 2008 alone, including the top spot which occurred on September 9, 2008, when the Dow dropped -777.68 points according to that same source.

If you look at the history of the Dow, we can glean all sorts of interesting information as we begin to correlate the rise and fall of that index with major events in the world—from wars to recessions to other major events. Tracking the Dow and/or stock market, in general, is a relatively safe way (albeit incomplete way) to gauge the health of the economy.

Operating in a fairly secure place like the NYSE means there's a much lower operation risk than would be the case otherwise. Furthermore, the stock market acts as both a primary market and a secondary market.

A **PRIMARY MARKET** allows companies to issue and sell equity (ownership in their company) via shares to the common public at-large through a process of **IPO**'s (initial public offerings), an activity that helps companies raise capital from investors, and ideally, turn a profit for them.

A **SECONDARY MARKET** is where investors buy and sell securities that they already own, which is the major difference between the two aforementioned terms.

The major reason people buy and sell securities is to earn money—and leverage their money to make more of it. To that end, the stock market continues to be tracked very closely, as you can imagine.

For example, between the Dow Jones, the Standard & Poor's 500 (S&P 500), and the NASDAQ, they have netted investors an average of 9.8% return since 1928.[i]

Specifically, the Dow has a long-term average of 10.18%. The NASDAQ (which consists of more than 2,500 companies) has had a long-term average of 9.53%, and the S&P has a long-term return rate of 7.36%.

Since about 2009, we've witnessed steady growth in terms of GDP and the markets. For example, please note the following chart from "Money Week."[j]

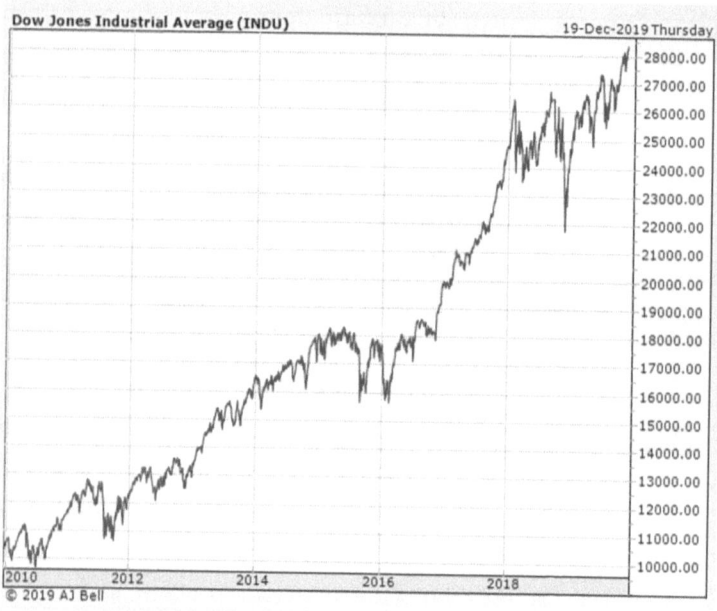

Dow Jones Industrial Average (INDU)   19-Dec-2019 Thursday

© 2019 AJ Bell

What does this all mean? Are things looking up? Is the economy in good shape today and in the years ahead?

It depends entirely on who you ask. If you're like Claudia's family, you do not have as much use for indices and exchanges, but shouldn't you?

People are getting rich off that measly 10% from making smart trades.

10% of $100 is only $10. But, at the same time, savvy investors have made millions or billions of dollars off that same 10%, primarily off what is called "the magic of compound interest."

Seasoned professional investors play the markets for years, and they have savvy people managing their money. And slowly, over time, given the proper moves (and compound interest), they make truckloads of cash.

When you're dealing with $1 million versus $100, for instance, that so-called measly 10% now comes to $100,000, and so you can see how a few percentage points here and there can make a world of difference.

In fact, according to Einstein, compound interest is the single most powerful force in the entire universe! It truly is "magical." The more frequently your money earns interest, the bigger your balance will grow because you're earning interest on the original balance plus the previously earned interest, so the growth is not linear.

Compound interest growth is exponential.

When interest is compounded, the amount paid in a year is more than the interest rate that's given, because there's another related term to consider, the **APY** (the annual percentage yield) when compound interest takes effect.

There are five main reasons that compound interest is so magical; let's look at all five.

There's the *initial investment*, the *monthly contribution*, the *length of savings*, the *interest rate*, and the *compound rate*.

The initial investment is the money you immediately put into an interest-bearing fund or account. The monthly contribution is the money you're going to add to your account each month (or each week) to build upon that initial investment. The length of savings is how long you plan on keeping your money in that account.

Of course, the longer you keep your money in the account, allowing interest to accumulate as more contributions are made, the more money you're going to earn. The interest rate is how much money your money earns over a given period of time, and those numbers vary, dependent on the investment opportunity.

Lastly, there's the compound rate, which is how often your interest compounds. It may compound daily, monthly, semiannually, or annually, and the more frequently your interest compounds, the more money you will make, especially in a strong economy.

Let's wrap up this section with a look at the Dow going all the way back to its inception. If you were to look really closely, you might notice drops and falls around the same time as major events—both globally and domestically.[k] Had this data continued, we would have noticed a steep dive in '08, for example.

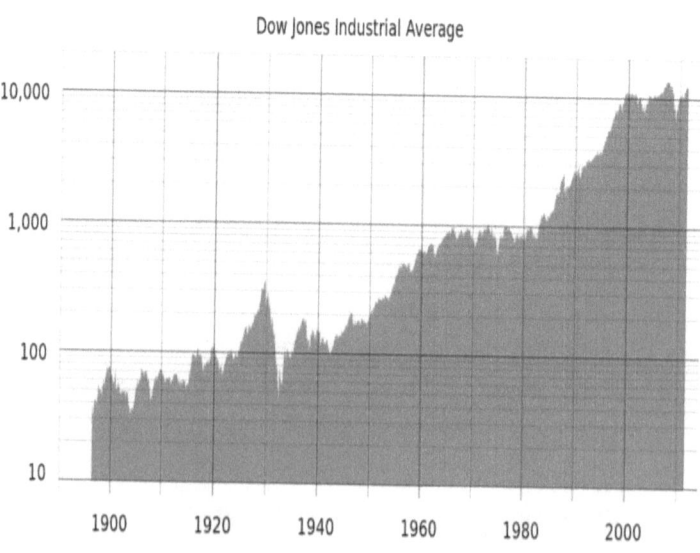

Dow Jones Industrial Average

REVIEW & REFLECT

Claudia had recently earned a raise, but nevertheless, she was not earning a whole lot of money overall. In fact, it might be easy to wonder how she would be able to invest any money at all in the first place—especially as she may have no "disposable" income to speak of.

She is also putting herself through school while working full-time as a hairdresser. After her meeting with Carson, she had a shift to cover and needed to hurry off.

Carson gladly gave her his card and escorted her to the door, secretly feeling fortunate to have made her acquaintance. No one ever met Claudia and wasn't instantly mesmerized.

"If you'd like to continue this discussion, as well as learn more about what we can do to put your money to work, please make an appointment soon."

"I think I've already learned more about the economy than I'd previously ever known."

"I'm glad to hear that, Claudia, and we will also discuss investment strategies, risk management, asset protection, college planning, retirement, and so forth, plus any questions you may have," he assured her.

"What if I don't have a lot of money?" she replied. "And what about student loans and that sort of thing?" she added with one foot out the door.

"I'm glad you asked," he replied. "We'll go over all of that in much more detail at our next meeting. In the meantime, don't worry yourself too much. If you decide to start investing, you don't have to start large," he added, opening the door.

"In fact, you can start pretty small for now with low contributions and a good, non-aggressive fund and then gradually over time increase your contributions once you're making more money. Or, come to think of it, there are even some new apps available I'll gladly tell you more about, too," he added, looking across the office as if what he was saying was completely sacrilegious.

"Now, that's a great idea," she replied. "I may not be a savvy investor yet, but I can definitely handle pretty much any app you throw at me."

"Just keep in mind," he continued. "The longer you put off beginning to invest your money, the more money you're missing out on for your future. Not to mention, the whole way you manage your money is equally—if not more important—than investing it, and there's a lot more I'd like to go over with you."

He paused and then continued, "I'll tell you what. If you come back, the coffee's on me, and there's this great little spot right here in this mall—plus an absolutely magical fountain we can sit at and talk."

Claudia was excited and agreed to meet with Carson the following day, before finally hurrying off for her pending shift on the other side of town.

Chapter 3
The Basics of Investing

OVERVIEW

We have heard the term middle-class a lot thus far and will be using it even more as we move along. To piggy-back off some concepts discussed in the opening pages, let's look at the following chart from My Budget 360 before jumping into a basic overview of investing now that we have more of a foundation of the market.[1]

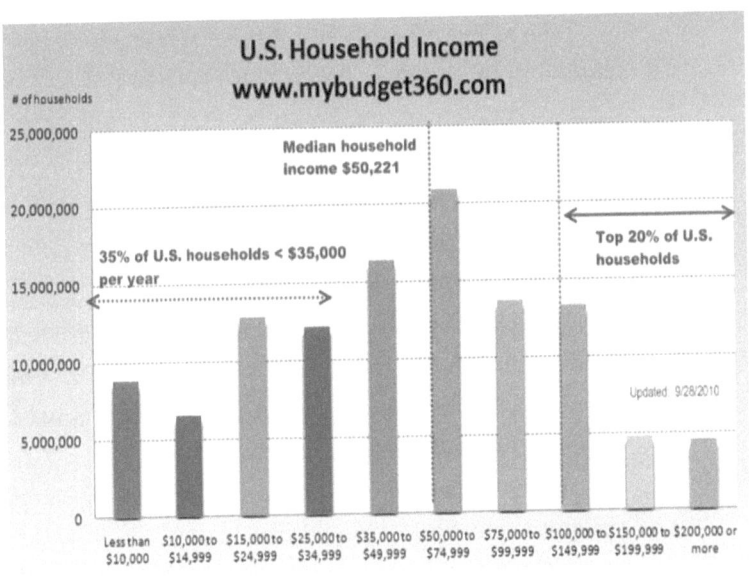

The Pew Research Center (Pew) defines the middle-class as being within 67% to 200% of the median household income.[m]

Think of it as a range of numbers where some people earn less than the median (at the low end), and others earn roughly twice as much (on the high end).

The Pew further categorizes household earning between $41,119 and $122,744 in 2017 as being "middle-class."

Now, if we look at the Census Bureau's official governmental numbers, the median household income in America in 2018 was $61,372.[n] For easy math, we'll say $60,000, and that figure hasn't changed much as of the time of writing this book.

According to that, our fictional character, Claudia, actually earns roughly one-half of the median household income in the US ($30,000 versus $60,000).

To be fair, Claudia still resides at home with her parents, although she certainly hopes that won't be the case for long.

Contrast that figure with the fact she's taking junior college courses, faced with stagnant wage growth and inflation, hyperinflating college costs, and more, and it's easy to see why affording college without going into debt seems like a real threat for her.

To place her earnings, $30,000, alongside other earners in this country, her income represents roughly 64% of the current US median income of about $47,060 (not to be confused with household income).[o]

At the same time, she does not fall into the category of poverty according to our sources.

According to Census, the federal poverty level for 2018 was $12,940 for one person, $16,910 for two people, $21,330 for three people, and $25,750 for a household of four, which is a strikingly low set of numbers.[p]

Perhaps, the following chart tells the tale of poverty better (as they say, a picture is worth a thousand words).[q] Poverty rates, per this official government source, were steadily declining up until about the time the US government actually declared war on poverty during the Johnson administration. We can philosophize why that is, but that's not within our purview.

U.S. Poverty Rate: 1959 to 2009

+3.8%
1978-83

+1.8%
2007-09

Source: Census Bureau

Claudia's household consists of six people (herself, her three siblings, and two parents), three of whom are working; and so, Claudia and her family do not fit the definition of poverty, but they easily fit our definition of "middle-class," but, according to our research, her household size is roughly double average.

Please refer to the following chart for more information (noting the steady decrease in household sizes over the previous decades).[r]

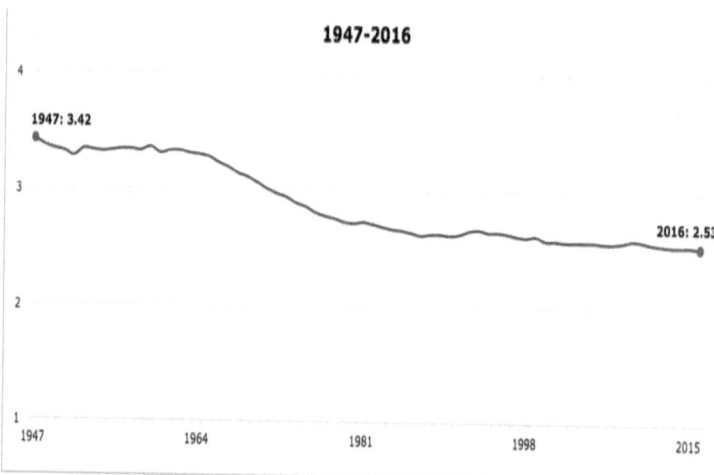

1947-2016

1947: 3.42

2016: 2.53

There are numerous reasons why household size is continuing to decrease as more and more Americans are postponing marriage into later in life or not getting married altogether, stagnate wage growth demanding two earners in a household, and more.

Plus, the whole definition of marriage (fortunately) and the ways people look at the institution of marriage is changing.

In the following sections, we will reintroduce our characters again before diving headlong into some of the basics of investing as it pertains to the US.

Once we have a better understanding of some of the associated terms and concepts better, we will no doubt be better equipped to wield the new-found techniques (as laid out in subsequent chapters) more effectively.

THE SECOND MEETING

Claudia had her first day off in weeks and was eager to learn all she could from her new financial advisor, Carson.

"Good afternoon," she said, extending her hand toward Carson.

Carson grabbed her hand and shook it vigorously and then asked her to have a seat in his office once more to finish going over a few more foundational concepts.

"I'm so glad you made it today," he acknowledged as they both took their seats across from one another.

"What will we be discussing?" she asked, seemingly ready and eager to sponge-up all the info she could.

"I thought we would talk about the various types of investments such as stocks, bonds, mutual funds, and a few other concepts first," he replied. "Oh, and if we have time, we'll also cover annuities, certificates, and retirement plans. These are all different ways to invest your money—and understanding the similarities and differences between each will be critical as we transition into more specific advice."

"Retirement plans?" she asked puzzled. "I'm not going to lie. I'm young and healthy. I haven't given retirement as much a thought as maybe I should. Is that important, too?"

"You bet!" he said more animated than ever. "It's never too early to start planning for retirement. In fact, I've had several middle-class clients over the years who have managed to retire millionaires by making all the right decisions in their youth. And let me tell you," he added, motioning with his hands, which bore the traces of age and experience. "They didn't earn a lot of money either."

Claudia was getting more excited by the minute with the innumerable possibilities. And in the following section, we take a look at some of the topics they covered.

STOCKS, BONDS, MUTUAL FUNDS & ETFs

Let's start with some basic definitions (you may always refer to the appendices for more details later). A stock is a type of security. If you've ever spoken with someone like Carson, you know that financial analysts are always saying, "Diversify, diversify, diversify," and there's a very good reason.

But what are we diversifying? Mainly, they're referring to the difference between stocks and bonds—but there are many other ways to diversify your investment portfolio. We'll be addressing more of this in our risk overview later, but let's begin with stocks and bonds.

STOCKS are one type of **SECURITY**, and there are many types of securities available. Generally speaking, a stock is an individual share in a particular company that is publicly traded.

Here's how it works: a company goes through a start-up phase early-on and try to raise some funds (where only "accredited investors" can invest, as noted earlier, unless it's a crowdfunding campaign, an entirely different concept). Those startups then enter an initial public offering (or IPO) where their securities can be publicly traded.

The company is hoping to expand and take on more money, so they make stocks in their company pubic for buying and selling, and they do that by splitting their entire company into shares.

They then sell those shares in that IPO or subsequent trading in either a primary or secondary market (defined in our glossary).

BONDS are totally different and represent debt. A prominent example of bond buying and selling occurs with governments.

For example, the US government sells its debt to pre-approved investors via US Treasury Bonds. That's one major example of bonds. They are not alone in doing this, as many countries raise money through the issuance of debt in this manner.

As far as companies, the whole process is simpler but occurs in a similar fashion.

Every bond has a specific, pre-set value and maturity. For instance, a $100 bond (for easy math) with a 5% coupon would pay $5 per year (generally in two payments of $2.50).

The preset timeframe, or **MATURITY**, is when the individual investor is owed the original principal of the bond except in the unusual circumstance the bond issuer **DEFAULTS** (when he/she is unable to repay the debt).

There are credit rating systems for various bondholders just like there are credit rating systems for consumers that track credit scores on the individual level. The higher an entity's credit rating, the greater the likelihood is they will repay their obligations.

Traditionally, buying bonds is a safe way to earn money, albeit the return on most bonds is not high.

Similarly, when an investor buys stock in a company, they're buying ownership in that company and look to make money. If the company does well, the value of that stock will rise, netting a profit for the investor.

However, there are a number of risks involved with buying stocks because what if a company does not perform well? As you can imagine, the value goes down, netting a loss for the investor—which is something that happens a lot.

The more you know about investing, the more likely you are to make wise investments, and there are numerous categories of risk we'll get into later.

However, let's say stocks generally have a higher return power than bonds under most circumstances.

In addition to stocks and bonds, there are many other investment options, including **EXCHANGE-TRADED FUNDS (ETFs)** and **MUTUAL FUNDS,** which are generally much safer than individual stocks or bonds.

Exchange-traded funds involve a collection of securities such as stocks that track an underlying index, and they commonly invest in various sectors and employ a number of different strategies.

On that note, a **MARKET INDEX** is a hypothetical portfolio of investment holdings that represent a segment of a **FINANCIAL MARKET.**

The calculation of the index comes from the prices of the underlying holdings, and some indices have values based on market-cap weighting (the value of a company), revenue-weighting, float-weighting, and fundamental-weighting, so there are various methodologies employed to determine the impact of an item within an index.[s]

ETFs and mutual funds share some similarities, but in general, an ETF is a collection of securities that are traded on an exchange (similar to stock), so their prices fluctuate up and down all day long while the ETF is being bought and sold on an exchange such as the S&P.

In fact, the whole reason it's called an exchange-traded fund is that it's traded on an exchange.

ETFs offer an array of investment types, including stocks, commodities, and bonds, and some (not all) offer only US holdings, for example. They also offer low expense ratios and fewer broker commissions than buying stocks individually, which makes them great investment opportunities for new investors—in this author's opinion.

When we get into the chapter on Fintech, we will explore a number of new and clever ways to trade ETFs, stocks, bonds, and mutual funds.

In the meantime, there are various types of ETFs to discuss, namely Bond ETFs, Industry ETFs, Commodity ETFs, Currency ETFs, and so-called Inverse ETFs.

One of the biggest advantages of ETFs is that they offer a lower average cost because it would be prohibitively expensive for an investor to buy all the stocks one ETF holds, and it's just much easier, as you can imagine because an investor only needs to make one transaction to trade an ETF versus countless ones with trading stocks.

This leads to lower commissions, naturally, and the expense ratios are typically further lowered because of how they track a particular index (i.e., the S&P).

Because they're so easily tracked, it's a great entry-level investment for newer investors who are just getting their feet wet in the markets and looking for something they can easily understand—and yet, still make money at.

Not all ETFs are passively traded and there are options for more actively managed ETFs with higher fees, but those are used for specific industries.

If you are knowledgeable about a certain industry—or are more prone toward one over others—actively managed

ETFs might be a great investment strategy for you, once you are all set and more comfortable.

Regardless of which investment style you prefer, the important thing to note is how your fund is managed, the resulting expense ratio (the costs involved), and as with any investment, you will want to weigh those costs against your rate of return and your appetite for risk and make sure it's worth holding.

Another advantage of holding ETFs in the **DIVIDENDS**. ETFs are not alone in offering dividends—but some investments do not offer those at all, and it's a great way to have some liquidity with your investments.

Dividends are officially considered the distribution of a reward from a portion of a company's earnings which are paid to shareholders and taxed much differently than conventional earned income (defined later).

How those funds are allocated depends on the board of directors for the company, although they must be approved through shareholders with **VOTING RIGHTS**.

Dividends can be offered as cash, shares of stock, or other property.

Mutual funds are not entirely unlike ETFs and are one of the most common types of investments. Mutual funds are a type of financial vehicle made up of a pool of money collected from numerous individual investors in securities (such as stocks and bonds), and they are managed by professional money managers.

Those managers allocate the fund's assets and try to produce **CAPITAL GAINS** for the investors in a pool.

In this sense, mutual funds are great, because they give small investors proportional access to professionally ran portfolios and money managers, further alleviating risk.

These funds invest in an array of security types, and their performance is tracked as the change in **MARKET CAPITALIZATION** (or **MARKET CAP)**, which is the total market value of a company's outstanding shares of stock.

In other words, the market cap is how much a company is worth—or it's one way of determining a company's value based on the cost of its stocks and how many shares there are of that stock.

Mutual funds are tracked per market cap and are divided into different categories based on the types of securities they represent. These funds charge fees (called expense ratios) and, in some cases, commissions, so its incumbent on individual investors to determine the various type of funds available, the costs involved, and weigh those costs alongside their own appetite for risk.

Even though mutual funds are tracked by market cap, the exact price of a mutual fund share is referred to as **NET ASSET VALUE** (NAV) or (NAVPS) which is derived by dividing the total value of the securities in a portfolio by the total amount of shares outstanding (outstanding shares are held by individual investors, institutional investors, company officers, etc.).

The average fund holds hundreds or more securities—and the value in that is, again, "Diversification, diversification, diversification."

Let's now address some other common types of investments before concluding this section with an overview of retirement and Social Security.

ANNUITIES & CERTIFICATES

Annuities and certificates of deposits are other types of investments, and they are crucial to properly planning for retirement. There are a number of similarities with each one, as well as some differences.

ANNUITIES are issued by insurance companies. **CERTIFICATES OF DEPOSIT** or **CDs**, on the flip side, are issued by lenders such as banks, savings and loan companies, and credit unions, all with the distinct purpose of raising funds—and subsequently, potentially netting a return for individual investors.

The most common annuities are **FIXED ANNUITIES** and **VARIABLE ANNUITIES**, and as you can expect, there are differences between the two, but both are created by an investor who is literally depositing his or her money into an insurance company (annuities are not associated with banks).

The main difference between the two types of annuities is in the type of return an investor can expect. With fixed annuities, a specific, pre-set, agreed upon return is stated along with periodic payments over a period of time, which is also pre-set.

What makes variable annuities trickier is that they take the money that's deposited and then reinvest that money and try to make a profit for both the issuer and the investor who's money they are literally playing with.

All these practices are tightly governed by the SEC and there are other types of annuities but fixed and variables are the major two types.

One variation would be what's known as an **INDEXED ANNUITY**, which is involved in other investments in a particular index (i.e., S&P 500), and these annuities do not commonly fall within the realm of SEC protection.

Fixed annuities do not fall within the SEC's guidelines. Indexed annuities commonly do not fall within the SEC's guidelines. But variable annuities do fall within the SEC's guidelines, as they are riskier than fixed ones.

CDs are different from an annuity, primarily based on the type of issuer. To recap, annuities are offered by insurance companies, whereas CDs are offered by lenders such as banks, savings and loan companies, and other lenders.

Here's how CDs generally work: an investor agrees to deposit a certain sum of money within a financial institution for a set amount of time (generally ranging from one month to five years or longer depending on the type of CD and the lender institution).

The institution provides a set rate of interest to the investor, so in this regard, CDs are less risky than say a variable annuity, which is tightly controlled.

When a CD matures (when it reaches its lifespan), the investor will receive the full amount of her investment. She will also receive any accumulated unpaid interest.

The great thing about CDs is that you can buy them — and forget about them (essentially).

They accrue a fixed rate over time, and they are generally considered to be one of the safest investments you can make, albeit they do not tend to net the biggest returns.

A person's appetite for risk is directly tied to the type of investment she should be making—and how much they'd like to make versus how much, if any, they can stand to lose. In the case of CDs, investors do not have to worry about a total loss, for instance.

CDs and annuities do have some similarities, too. Namely, both CDs and annuities have penalties associated with withdrawing money early. However, many annuities available today offer periodic payments, and so that's something you would want to know about prior to investing in one of those.

What is my rate of return? Is it fixed or variable? When does my CD or annuity mature? And so, those are a few more of the questions you would want to use when discussing investments of that nature with an advisor.

Now that we have a better understanding of some of the more common types of investing, it's good to know in what ways we should be planning for our inevitable retirements, as well, as those are two very different things.

The whole way we invest day-to-day will be much different than how we plan for retirement, although both strategies should align with one another.

RETIREMENT PLANS

TRADITIONAL IRAs and **401(k)s** are the most common type of retirement accounts, and in this section, we'll briefly address the different types of accounts available today.

We'll begin with IRAs, then 401(k)s, before making a few brief suggestions concerning **SOCIAL SECURITY** along with some general advice on retirement planning.

Some employers offer retirement plans—and if yours does not, we strongly advise creating one of your own and/or positioning yourself for future years where you can have an employer who will contribute toward your retirement as much as possible.

Retirement investments and accounts ensure you have enough money for all your expenses long after you stop working.

As in the case of Claudia's parents, they have not or been able to plan for retirement, and she would like to position herself differently and plan for her future.

How you plan for retirement depends on your lifestyle, as well. Let's face it, some people burn through money much faster than others and live entirely different lives (it doesn't mean they're happier. It just means they spend more money).

The whole structure of your retirement must be devised ahead of time—to those ends—so that you can rest assured that whatever goals you have are met. So, that's the first part.

You should also be setting goals for yourself with the kind of money you will need for retirement. Will you own a home by then? Will you still be paying on your mortgage? Are you one of the more and more Americans who do not plan on ever buying a home? Will you be needing to continue making rent payments? What about other expenses?

Next, understand that a trained financial planner can guide you through your investment and retirement goals. He or she will understand economic trends on the macro level, yield rates, historical references, and your specific circumstances.

Retirement money is generally divided between accounts, one of which is called an **INDIVIDUAL RETIREMENT ACCOUNT** or IRA, which is a tax-advantaged investing tool that individuals use to earmark funds for retirement.

There are numerous types of IRAs, such as Traditional IRAs, Roth IRAs, SEP IRAs, and SIMPLE IRAs.

Investments held in an IRA can encompass a range of products from bonds, stocks, ETFs, and mutual funds, and a self-directed IRA can be both traditional and Roth. Self-directed IRAs allow investors to make decisions and gives them better access to a broader range of investments—including real estate and other investments.

In Claudia's case, she is an individual investor (or about to become one), so she would likely be steered toward a Traditional IRA or Roth IRA.

On the other hand, small businesses and self-employed individuals set up SEP and SIMPLE IRAs. These accounts are set up by IRS approved institutions and include banks, credit unions, savings and loan associations, and brokerages, the latter of which is where most investors set up their IRAs.

The following chart is not guaranteed for 100% accuracy but has been crafted utilizing the latest numbers.

	Traditional IRA	Roth IRA	SEP IRA	SIMPLE IRA	401(k) / 403(b)
Annual contribution limit	$5,500 if you're under 50; $6,500 if you're 50 or older	$5,500 if you're under 50; $6,500 if you're 50 or older	25% of earnings, up to $54,000	$12,500 if you're under 50; $15,500 if you're 50 or older	$18,000 if you're under 50; $24,000 if you're 50 or older
Earliest withdrawal age to avoid penalties	59-½ (exceptions apply)	59-½ for earnings portion; principal contributions can be withdrawn at any time	59-½ (exceptions apply)	59-½ (exceptions apply)	59-½ (exceptions apply)
Required minimum distributions	Starting at 70-½	No required minimum distribution	Starting at 70-½	Starting at 70-½	Starting at 70-½
Taxes on contributions	Contributions are made with pre-tax dollars	Contributions are made with after-tax dollars	Contributions are made with pre-tax dollars	Contributions are made with pre-tax dollars	Contributions are made with pre-tax dollars
Taxes on withdrawals	Withdrawals are taxed as ordinary income	Withdrawals are tax-free	Withdrawals are taxed as ordinary income	Withdrawals are taxed as ordinary income	Withdrawals are taxed as ordinary income

Please note that you cannot invest in an IRA with **SOCIAL SECURITY BENEFITS**, child support, or certain other types of income. According to the IRS, investments in IRA accounts actually have to be made via **TAXABLE EARNED INCOME** only.

Some examples of approved taxable income include wages, salaries, and tips (an employer pays), union strike benefits, long-term disability benefits received before the minimum retirement age, net earnings from self-employment.

Here's a brief look at **UNAPPROVED EARNED INCOME**: pay received for work while in a penal institution, interest, dividends, Social Security or other retirement income, unemployment benefits, alimony, or child support.

For a full look at which types of incomes are approved—and which ones are not—refer to the following endnote at your leisure.[t]

Before determining which IRA suits you and what types of income can be used, again, we advise speaking with a financial advisor such as Carson (from our fictional example).

A 401(k) is a different type of retirement account with different rules than IRAs (we've denoted other differences between the two in the last chart).

If you have retired recently or changed jobs, you may have a number of questions about what to do with your money in your employer's 401(k) plan; however, typically, you have four options. When it comes to these types of accounts, you may either *take it, leave it, move it,* or *roll it over.*

If you leave it in the former employer's account, you need to refer to the exact terms in your plan. Some plans offer educational materials, planning tools, telephone and/or online help guides, workshops, or other forms of help to steer you along.

To move your money, you may have to meet certain requirements before doing so—again, dependent on the exact plan, and you'll want to read all the details closely.

One of the more ideal moves is to roll the account over, and generally, that's allowed as long as you meet certain guidelines.

One option might be to consolidate your retirement accounts, which is something I might advise—dependent on the individual's unique circumstances.

Lastly, if you take the money, just understand that you're subject to tax consequences, as these plans are not fully mature until, generally, the investor reaches the age of 70 ½, and once again, please refer to the aforementioned chart.

Social Security is another form of retirement, and the one that most people are familiar with. A lot of people, sadly, are fully reliant on Social Security benefits or planning to allow themselves to become fully reliant on them later in life.

When the SS Trust was first introduced in 1935, however, it was never intended as a primary source of income to support a person or household during retirement. It was merely a safety net for people who were unable to secure sufficient retirement savings otherwise.

Nowadays, more and more Americans are paying attention to their Social Security planning, and it's becoming a vital element of a larger retirement plan.

Before wrapping up this, let's look at a few tips that will help maximize your social security benefits, as well as the following chart noting the ages you can receive your benefits per the Social Security Administration's guidelines.[u]

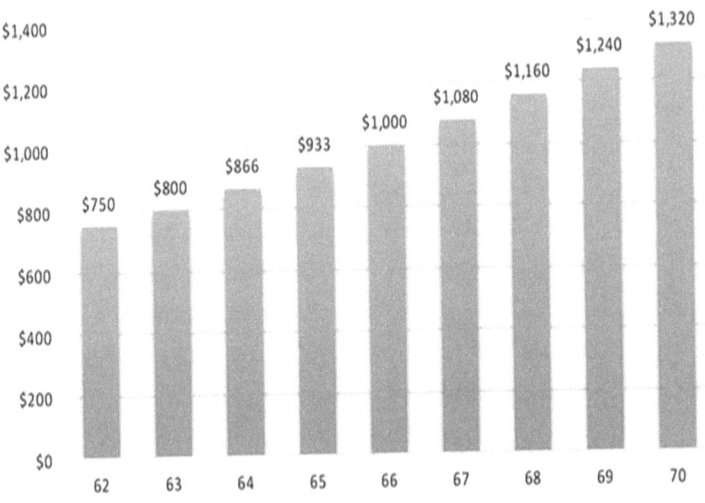

If you can work 35 years or more, it will help ensure that you get the most benefits calculable under the current guidelines. The key is to earn as much money as you can before retirement in order to maximize said benefit. If you do retire early (through disability or whatever the reason), you will not receive your maximum benefit, whereas waiting until age 70 to claim can increase your benefit by as much as 8% per year beyond full retirement age; also, be advised that as much as 85% of your benefits may be subject to federal taxes if you are at a certain income level after first receiving your social security.

Our hope is that you will not rely solely on social security for retirement—and that you will take advantage of other investment and retirement options, many of which are notated herein.

As far as Claudia, it became increasingly clear during her second meeting with her adviser, that she still had more questions than answers. Let's check back in.

REVIEW & REFLECT

"In your case, Claudia," Carson said. "Navigating retirement as a new citizen can prove particularly challenging, but the good news is that you do qualify for benefits."

"I'm actually surprised to hear that," she relented. "I am only recently a US citizen, and I paid a lot of taxes before becoming a citizen, actually. Wouldn't I lose those benefits?"

"While it's true that non-citizens must meet certain criteria outlined by the SSA to qualify for social security benefits, non-US citizens who are living legally in the US and who have earned benefits can collect social security under several conditions."

"I didn't know that."

"A lot of people do not—and often, my fear is that they're too afraid to even ask, which is a travesty. If you worked, you should be entitled to receive benefits—but understandably, it's on a case by case basis."

"I understand," she quipped. "And some of this information I will be sharing with my parents," she added.

"Generally speaking, if they have an assigned social security number and are legally permitted to work here, then they would be eligible for benefits," he added. "And from I understand, they meet those criteria, but I'd love to speak with them, as well, someday."

"But one thing I would like to reiterate in the meantime," he added. "Our goal is that we do not want them nor you to have to solely rely on social security. The fact is the whole social security program is potentially in trouble given the latest trends. If Congress doesn't act soon, we may have a massive liquidity problem on our hands.

The social security liquidity crisis will only be further exacerbated in the coming years as more and more elderly hit the roles."

Carson seemed concerned, as did Claudia. He then added, "We'd like to forego any chances of you having to rely on those benefits even though we may stay optimistic that they'll be there when needed. So, I'd like to help you structure a much stronger, more diversified retirement plan."

"I'm so glad I came here today, and my mind is already at ease just with everything we've already discussed. I've already learned so much—and I look forward to seeing what some of the advice will be for me specifically when it comes to my retirement, investing, and plans for my business moving forward," she added. "In fact, I'm totally reevaluating so many things already."

"What are some of the other things we learned today?"

"I never realized there were so many different types of retirement accounts for starters," she jokingly replied. "Just with IRA's, for example, there are many types."

"And we only covered some of the most common ones. The fact is, there are numerous ways to plan for a person's retirement, but I do hope this information helps. But there's still so much more that I'd like to discuss with you if you have the time in the coming days."

"I would like that very much," she replied, standing up and offering her hand across the table.

"In fact, there are some great tips concerning financial technology apps that I think would be right up your alley," he added. "Or, some specific types of investments we could broker for you here. Plus, we still haven't discussed college planning—or gotten that cup of coffee we mentioned before."

Claudia and Carson agreed to meet again the next time she had a day off—the following week. She was continuing to work long hours in the salon while taking courses at the community college and helping out with her younger siblings at home.

Chapter 4
Fintech & the Future of Investing

OVERVIEW

After discussing our key pillars, meeting our fictional character, Claudia, and then launching into the basics of investing, we will begin examining modern trends, and the way financial tech apps ("Fintech") are shaping the very fabric of the way people invest and manage their money.

Please note, when we say Fintech, we are describing new technology that is improving people's lives and automating the way financial services are being delivered.

Fintech is utilized to help individuals and companies better manage their financial operations, processes, and lives by utilizing new software that can be accessed via computers—and smartphones.

Needless to say, if you're one of the millions of Americans who are feeling broke and broken, Fintech may become one part of the solution you'll want to work towards.

In recent years, the term Fintech has been used for mostly consumer-oriented purposes and includes sectors and industries such as education, retail banking, fundraising and nonprofits, and investment management, to name a few.

Fintech includes the development and usage of cryptocurrencies such as bitcoin.

While Fintech is an exciting new trend that's putting more tools in the hands of consumers, as of yet, the largest part of the financial market still lies in traditional sources such as banking and other institutions.

At the same time, most Fintech companies are similar to the companies they're trying to disrupt in their respective spaces. For instance, for consumers with poor credit, there's an app called "Tala" who offers consumers in the developing world microloans by doing a deep data dive on their phones for their transaction history, what games they play, and other unconventional factors.

Tala states their goal is to give consumers better options than local banks—and predatory lenders, which have come about in recent years with exorbitant interest rates once banks started getting out of the signature loan game.

So-called "Payday Loan," "Title Loan," and other nefarious lenders offer consumers loans (typically up to $2,500) with interest rates that often exceed 400%.

Consumers can place the title on their car down as collateral (for some lenders, they even use consumer electronics and other goods as collateral). Please note, we could not discourage using Payday or Title Loan companies enough.

Other lenders in this category require no collateral but still charge incredibly high-interest rates. Because these types of companies are coming under fire more and more in recent years with all new regs, companies like Tala have spotted a niche and are attempting to leverage that for their success.

A loan originator called "Upstart" wants to make FICO obsolete by using different data sets to determine creditworthiness and includes particulars such as employment history, education, and whether a would-be borrower can accurately relay to them their credit score to decide whether to write loans and the terms of those loans.

Another example of Fintech is called Robinhood. It is a mobile-only stock trading app that charges no fees for trades, and peer-to-peer lending sites promise lower rates by expanding competition for loans to broaden market forces and bring prices and other competitive advantages to consumers in the crowded space.

If you're wondering where this leaves traditional institutions, imagine the company Walmart for example. Amazon was a massive disruptor and offered retail services and delivery, which was nothing more than a novel idea when it originated; of course, Amazon has exploded in growth in recent years.

Traditional brick and mortar stores like Walmart finally got into deliveries, as well, albeit only recently. Walmart execs finally sensed the changing tides of the economy and started offering services like curbside grocery pickup, and in some locations, home deliveries.

A similar occurrence is happening in traditional banking. For example, in 2016, Godman Sachs, a massive name on Wallstreet, launched a consumer lending platform called "Marcus" to compete with other Fintech companies in that space—and broaden their own **VALUE PROP** (what value they bring to the market).

As you can see, the term "financial technology" can apply to any innovation in how people transact business from the invention of digital money such as Bitcoin to bookkeeping services to money transfer apps to investing spare change with Acorns to many others.

The whole way people invest, trade, and budget money is rapidly changing, and if you're feeling broke and broken, a thorough dive into all that Fintech offers will no doubt ease the feelings of disenfranchisement, as you learn exciting new ways to manage your money.

In the following sections, we'll only focus on what we found to be the three most important areas of Fintech for our purposes, namely investing, trading, and budgeting.

We cover each one in more detail in the following sections, before rounding out this chapter with some thoughts on the future of investing and Fintech and where that leaves traditional investors—and new ones.

INVESTING WITH FINTECH

Matador is an app for socialized investing, meaning it functions as a cross between Facebook and Robinhood. You can connect with your friends, see how they're investing, follow their lead if you choose, and it allows free trading of stocks and ETFs, so there are both components.

With Matador, you have all the information needed to trade, research companies, view stock prices, and network while you're at it!

This book is not meant to construe any direct financial advice (as all individual's circumstances are different), but I can honestly say that even though I come from a strong background of trading with Merrill and Morgan Stanley, I have been pleased to see Matador and other apps burst onto the scene.

Bundil is another interesting mobile app as it allows investors to invest their spare change from everyday credit or debit card purchases into crypto, but for the average new investor, crypto may seem overwhelming and wrought with risk.

Bundil seeks to remove the barriers to investing by simply rounding up purchases and automatically investing the difference in cryptocurrency. If this sounds familiar, there's another app that allows users to round-up and invest their "spare change," which has gotten much more notoriety in recent years with celebrity spokespeople.

Acorns Invest (or "Acorns") automatically invest your spare change and lets you invest as little as $5 anytime or on a recurring basis into a portfolio of ETFs (which we covered in a previous chapter).

Using ETFs, your investments are then diversified across thousands of different stocks and bonds. There is another platform by Acorns called Acorns Later, too, which is an IRA account and allows investors to save for retirement by setting easy recurring contributions.

When you sign up, the app recommends the right IRA for you based on your goals, current employment, and income levels (there's also an Acorns Spend checking and debit account where you can save and invest while you spend).

When Acorns talks about "spare change," they are talking about "rounding-up" your debit and credit card purchases, a revolutionary idea. Your purchase of $1.27 is rounded up to the next dollar, so you're checking/debit account is charged $0.73, and that money goes into a linked account (such as an Acorns Later or Acorns Invest account).

If you set up recurring investments, it will allow you to invest as little as $5 per day, week, or month, and you can make one-time investments anytime to boost your account value, in case you're wondering if investing "loose change" adds up to anything.

In fact, it does. Through the magic of compound interest and having access, albeit indirectly, to professionally managed ETFs, and having the ability to give your account a boost with occasional one-time payments, you would be shocked how much money you can invest over a period of time. I wanted to know the answer to that exact question myself during the construction of this book, and so I consulted a number of resources to find out before investing in Acorns or recommending it to my followers and readers.

According to the Acorns site, the Found Money Program is a means of having the opportunity to "cash forward" versus traditional credit card "cash back," and it turns out that Acorns has a pretty impressive network of partners, featuring prominent brands like Barnes and Noble, Airbnb, Blue Apron, Expedia, Groupon, Walmart, Nike, Sephora, Lyft, DirecTV, and more.

Acorns is clearly at the cutting edge of the Fintech industry and simplifies the entire process of investing through it's Found Money Program, where you get a percentage back on your purchases through its network of partners that are automatically added to your account (or "wallet").

In addition to Found Money, your "loose change" is rounded up, and so it's an impressive framework for investing, especially when you can also make one-time contributions as much as you want.

This option could be a great opportunity for anyone feeling broke and broken who's interested in starting to invest but not sure which way to turn.

With Acorns, all you have to do is link a credit or debit card and start shopping. The whole guesswork and confusion that's often associated with investing are alleviated, and you have the opportunity to passively earn extra money.

The key point when using Acorns, or other Fintech, is patience. You're not going to go from broke and broken to a millionaire overnight. But it's potentially one aspect of a broader plan for investing and saving for retirement—that will indeed take some time.

Safeguarding your future isn't a quick process, but what we've found with most new investors, is that once they start seeing their portfolio grow (from say a few hundred dollars to a few thousands dollars or more), it begins to take a psychological toll as you move away from feeling broke to feeling hopeful and optimistic.

In addition to Acorns, there are a number of other great apps available today—but let's take a look at the ones associated with trading and budgeting.

TRADING WITH FINTECH

With Acorns and other Fintech apps, you can invest money— often just a little bit of loose change and augment that with one-time payments occasionally and watch your account grow.

But there are other apps available today that require a little more diligence. Let's now look at the popular trading platform known as Robinhood.

Robinhood is a free, US-based stock trading app that allows completely free stock trading, cryptocurrency, and ETF trades.

What makes Robinhood so popular its virtually free, as they charge zero commission fees and have zero account minimums making it ideal for young, new investors looking to get started.

As of 2019, Robinhood had already emerged as the largest US-based online stockbroker, surpassing E-Trade in recent months. It is known as a broker-dealer app and allows trades commission-free; however, Robinhood does not currently offer any tax-sheltered accounts like IRAs and other types of retirement accounts.

You can trade stocks, ETFs, **REITs** (defined in our glossary), options, and cryptos. If you upgrade to Robinhood Gold, you can even take part in **MARGIN TRADING** and that platform has seen meteoric growth over the past year.

Because Robinhood is a new technology, a lot of customers worry if it's safe, and as always, we do advise at least speaking with a trained professional and/or doing your homework before starting; of course, merely reading this book is one big step in the right direction, and I believe a person can do well on Robinhood.

Robinhood is protected by something called the *Securities Investor Protection Corporation* (SIPC) for up to $500,000 for securities and up to $250,000 for cash claims, plus Robinhood is regulated by the *Financial Industry Regulatory Authority* (FINRA), which makes Robinhood vastly safer to use than many other apps—in this author's opinion.

Opening an account with Robinhood is different than walking into a brokerage or financial advisor's office like Carson (from our example). It's much easier, although the app is required by law to collect certain amounts of information on its clients. For example, to file information tax forms, you must give them your social security number, and there's no way around that.

Not to mention, if you're new to investing and do not do your due diligence, assess your risk profile as noted earlier, or have trained guidance (at least in the early stages), it can be a recipe for disaster, so we encourage you to do your homework before using Robinhood or any other Fintech resource.

If it's something that does intrigue you, you can follow a few of the following tips.

First, simply load the app. Then, find your preferred stock, ETF, REIT, or cryptocurrency. Tap the "trade" button, and the next page will give you the option to either "buy" or "sell." Select the type of transaction you want to make and the number of shares you're transacting with and then confirm your order! After confirmation, submit the order, and you're all done!

You've made your first trade on Robinhood, and you can find their link in the endnotes here.[v]

Since its free, it's a very common question that's out there today is how they make money. Robinhood is actually good, in my opinion, at being transparent about how they make money. So, nothing is hidden that's going to shock you.

For example, they offer premium accounts like Robinhood Gold, which allows margin trading and other benefits—but it starts at only $5 per month, so it's still an affordable option.

Robinhood also makes money on margin interest, like any stockbroker, and earns interest from the piles of cash that its various users are depositing. They charge $10 for any trade made through a phone call, and they can assist you with purchasing foreign stocks for $35-$50.

So, those are the most common ways that Robinhood earns money, but they're good about being upfront and open with their pricing.

In addition to Robinhood, there are a number of other trading apps available, too—and our purpose was never to promote Robinhood (or anyone else) over others. And in addition to trading and investing apps, there are some great budgeting apps we will be discussing, too.

BUDGETING WITH FINTECH

Getting your finances on track is especially difficult when you're already feeling broken and broken, but it's going to take being proactive and diligent to pull yourself up and start heading in the right direction.

At the same time, we understand that all circumstances are different and want to encourage you to follow me on Instagram (@pedromfrias) and other platforms, where I keep my followers and readers up to date on the world of investing—and so much more.

Part of what we wanted to do herein was stress the importance of budgeting, and we hope this section sheds some light on the concept of saving and budgeting.

People have different techniques for handling how money comes and goes—and still, yet, other people don't track their expenses at all.

Tracking expenses starts with setting a budget—and trying to strictly adhere to it. One such app to help us do that is called Personal Capital, which includes budgeting, investment monitoring, and retirement goal-tracking.

After signing up for Personal Capital, you get retirement-focused info like your current age, when you plan to retire, and money you have in savings and investment accounts (if any). You can link those accounts that need to be managed—and get a great synopsis of where your money is going.

Personal Capital includes some great charts that make the whole budgeting process easier and that track your overall cash-flow from month to month, plus it's a good way to track whether or not you're on pace with your retirement goals or other long-term goals.

In addition to tracking your expenses, I also recommend **ANNUALIZING EXPENSES.**

We don't want to pitch any particular app—but we hope you will take advantage of one of them or track your expenses and budget in some other manner.

You Need a Budget is another option for you and also allows you to link your accounts and track where your money is going. Some people are more concerned about their personal information getting leaked out and/or shared with other vendors, and so You Need a Budget allows you to manually add transactions that way and avoid linking an account altogether.

YNAB connects with major banks and most other institutions, as well, and you can add cards and set specific goals for each account (like paying off a balance over a set amount of time or creating a budget which includes your entire balance).

After linking your accounts, you'll give every dollar in your accounts an assignment. YNAB calls this "giving every dollar a job" per their main website, which means you shouldn't have any leftover money after everything is assigned. When you do, those dollars should go toward either emergency savings, investments, or retirement contributions.

I like the idea of putting your money to work for you, and YNAB makes this easier than ever and makes sure you truly understand the value of having a budget and managing your money wisely.

YNAB even offers free workshops on budgeting, debt, savings, and other areas, and they have a big library of education resources, as well. It's also easy to use. After signing up, you can use the app for free for the first 34 days, and then, if you continue to use it, it only costs about $84 per year.

Again, this isn't a specific endorsement of YNAB or any other app, but I think it's a good deal. You can also choose to be billed a monthly amount of $6.99 if that's something you'd prefer versus paying the balance at one time.

If you'd like to give it a try, you can find a link to download YNAB at this endnote.[w]

There are too many budgeting apps to list, but another one we wanted to mention is called Mint.

Mint will help you set budgets, track your spending and link various accounts, and it makes sure you're paying your bills on time, which will no doubt improve your **FICO SCORES**.

Another great thing about the app is that it's intuitive, and that means the longer you use Mint, the more it learns about you and your particular preferences, which makes using it even easier.

With the app, you can recategorize expenses, when needed, split transactions (if you make a grocery list, you can split up where you'll be shopping into more than one place), and you can see your spending over time, which is crucial.

Recall we talked about annualizing your expenses, and the reason that's important is that you would be shocked how much money you may be spending on something as seemingly trivial as energy drinks.

You should be annualizing the costs of all common expenditures, no matter how small they may seem to be.

Let's say you drink 1-2 energy drinks on average (i.e., $3 per drink avg.). That's about $4.50 per day, which doesn't sound like a lot of money. In fact, you can probably find that much money under your couch cushions or in the tricky spot everything in your car disappears into.

But when you annualize the expense, it comes to $1,642.50! Can you believe it? If you drink 1 ½ energy drinks per day, on average, you're spending over $1,600 per year, and my experience has been, some people spend even more than that. Plus, they're incredibly unhealthy at the same time, so people are spending thousands of dollars per year on a very bad habit, frankly.

With Mint, you can track those expenses over a year and then compare what you actually spent versus what you were budgeting for (if you're budgeting for that kind of thing at all). Simply put, the money you spend throwing away on energy drinks could be easily used for something like Acorns or some other investment account. So, put your money to work!

Another feature you may enjoy with Mint is you can change your budget over time—the more and more you review your spending and make adjustments.

I must also point out, savings are not listed as a specific category on Mint, unfortunately, but you can manually add the category yourself and then mark that transfer accordingly.

You can also set goals on the app, which is my favorite feature. For instance, if you're paying off your student loan debt or moving out of your parent's home, you can set a specific goal for those things.

I shared a link to YNAB, so I will do so for Mint, as well, but again, this is not an endorsement of ANY app.[x]

In fact, I don't care which one you use, so long as you are doing the following:

1. Decide on a budgeting app like YNAB, Mint, etc.

2. Make clear-cut goals for yourself.

3. Annualize your expenses and start tracking your money coming in and out.

4. Put each dollar you spend to work by setting a zero balance budget where every dollar is earmarked.

5. Take anything that goes over those budgeted items and transfer into savings, retirement, or investing.

6. And create a specific category for savings, link an account, and start building a "rainy day" fund.

The aforementioned techniques will no doubt help you—and we'll certainly see what recommendations Carson has for our fictional friend, Claudia, in subsequent chapters.

However, in the meantime, let's take a look at market trends and what I'd simply call—the future of investing before proceeding.

THE FUTURE OF INVESTING

I often get asked, "What is the future of investing or where do you see the economy going," and I wanted to conclude this chapter with a general overview and some thoughts on those subjects.

The majority of my followers are millennials, and as we turn to the future, the very ground we're standing on is shifting beneath our feet. It's happening all the time.

It's no wonder some of my followers feel broke and broken when college isn't teaching us what we need to be hearing and everywhere we turn it seems like the only things we are hearing are all the negatives.

The biggest thing, for me, is that the financial industry is changing drastically, and in a few short years, the industry I worked for will look much different than before.

Large asset owners with in-house investing expertise will start to offer services more and more to smaller asset owners who are competing with traditional investment managers for new streams. For the investor, this increased competition should further bring costs down.

The heightened competition and acceleration of the adoption of new technologies will lead many traditional investors to become selective managers and leverage their scale for efficiencies and other benefits. In fact, institutional investor models are starting to mirror new technology startups already such as Mint and YNAB (to name a couple).

We are also likely to see hyper consolidation, which will create even larger firms in the future, but those firms will offer an array of services from consulting to investment to more and all at reduced costs. Declining prices will further put the squeeze on small money managers—but consumers should be mostly unaffected, and I'm confident options will remain aplenty.

Above all, the need to stay adaptable for consumers will be critical as the previously mentioned technologies take up larger places in the market.

In fact, this very book—the whole premise behind putting financial information into the hands of the masses will become increasingly more popular, as traditional investors consolidate and embrace newer technologies for themselves.

I'm also asked about **BLOCKCHAIN**—and no discussion on the future of investing would be complete without broaching the subject. Let's be clear: blockchain, AI, and other futuristic tech will drastically change the landscape from the top (institutional lenders and major investors) to everyday consumers who will struggle getting into the market and accessing all the right tools without proper education and support.

We see signs of implementation as of the writing of this book with traditional institutions believing blockchain will cut out the middleman and increase security and the efficiency of trading.

But some people believe it will take longer for these new technologies to gain traction. I believe that's not true and investors (seasoned and newer ones) will quickly adapt, as more and more startups look for frictionless transactions, which is the whole meaning of the game.

The main point of most new technologies is to make things as frictionless as possible—and consumer demand will further fuel this phenomenon.

The faster pace of the future markets will make faster decision-making more necessary, too, which will be fueled by new and enhanced quantitative approaches, fueling investments in startups and technology apps all geared around user-centered design.

The very thin advantage many asset managers have today will start fading more and more due to the aforementioned technology. To put this into a real-world perspective, we will return to our example with Claudia and Carson in subsequent sections—and see if any breakthroughs are starting to occur.

Please note, dear reader, I am not predicting the end to active money management—or any dire consequences for consumers.

The main point of this section is to demonstrate that the grounds are indeed changing—and the more you invest in yourself and the more you learn about the breadth of opportunities available, the better positioned you will be for the coming years.

This is important because social security is eroding as we see hyperinflation in an array of areas including education and healthcare, and more and more retirees will be hitting the rolls.

Where's this leave you?

Hopefully, more prepared than ever, and I certainly hope this message helps in some small way.

Let's now turn to the rising need for risk management and asset protection, two cornerstones of investing, which will no doubt stay equally (if not more) relevant in the coming years.

Chapter 5
Risk Management & Asset Protection

INTRO TO RISK MANAGEMENT

We often associate risk management with large corporations—but that's not the complete picture. Whether you're a seasoned pro or new to investing (like Claudia), an overview of risk management is needed to make informed decisions and understand how to protect one's assets moving forward.

Typically, investment risk is divided into two major categories: *systematic risk* and *non-systematic risk*. Systematic risk is associated with the overall market, whereas non-systematic risk is associated with individual players within that market.

NON-SYSTEMATIC RISK can be further broken down into business and industry risk; for example, if you buy common stock from Company X, you assume the risk associated with the specific company plus the risk of the industry in which the company operates.

The risk associated with the company involves such things as decisions made by management to the financial framework of the individual company. This is why **DUE DILIGENCE** when investing is particularly important, plus there are many other ways to mitigate risk.

It's also why a lot of people are leery about investing apps like say, Acorns, for example, but let's be clear. Those apps tend to buy ETFs which are exchange-traded funds, meaning they spread the risk out to practically zero.

Plus, with Acorns and similar Fintech apps, you get access to professional money managers with low-end contributions.

It's also simply untrue only savvy, seasoned investors need to concern themselves with risk.

Yes, the more actively you buy and sell stocks, bonds, and other securities, the more susceptible to risk you become. But understanding who you're actually investing and diversifying your holdings can reduce your risk to negligible numbers.

A more seasoned investor might, for example, find out all they can about a company they're investing in — and those companies who are being publicly traded have regular reporting requirements making matters easier.

This is one example of the due diligence we speak of. If a company assumes too much debt, for instance, a seasoned investor would be concerned about a drop in stock price and make a move ahead of the sell-off to protect herself against the threat.

Business risk constitutes a number of other factors, but for our purposes, that's a pretty good definition of business risk.

On the other hand, industry risk is also associated with the purchasing of a company's stock but implies the industry the company resides in. If the company is in healthcare, for example, and some new legislation was passed (as with the ACA years ago) that might affect the market, and if so, it's something the individual investor wants to understand.

The important thing to recall is that non-systematic risk (business and industry risk) can be almost entirely eliminated by diversification. That means you can lower if not zero-out your non-systematic risk by investing in numerous different companies and in numerous different industries so that you can eliminate any risk associated with any one particular company or sector.

Unfortunately, systematic risk cannot be zeroed-out because this type of risk is associated with a particular type of investment; for example, if you invest in the stock market, you are subjected to the risk associated with stocks, generally, and if you invest in bonds, you're subject to the risk of fluctuating interest rates in the bond market, generally, so systematic risk is not something that can be eliminated altogether.

To make life easier, in the following section, we notate the various types of risk to study—again, whether you're a seasoned investor or a newer one, these are things that you will absolutely want to become familiar with, and only the most common, most important types of risk were included for your convenience.

The main takeaway should be there are numerous types of risks and only some of those types can be fully mitigated, and the more you know about risk—and your own appetite for it—the better you will be able to navigate the world of investing like a professional money manager.

Moreover, understanding risk is one of the numerous key elements to going from broke and broken to a savvy investor—and it has everything to do with continuously investing in yourself, your own skillset, and your own knowledge.

MOST COMMON TYPES OF RISK

Risk management is the process of identifying, analyzing, and mitigating uncertainty for prospective investors against the potential for losses, and for professional, experienced investors, there are various types of risks they commonly familiarize themselves with.

Business Risk: a type of non-systematic risk associated with investing in a particular company. Needless to say, business risks can come in many forms, namely company debt and other issues common to specific companies. This type of risk is easily mitigated by diversifying in various types of companies. For example, let's say you put ALL your investing dollars into ONE company, Company Z. If Company Z goes belly up, what's that mean for your money? This is precisely why we encourage diversification and increasing your knowledge.

Credit Risk: a type of systematic risk associated with the overall creditworthiness of the company issue a particular bond. US-backed bonds, for example, have low to zero credit risk. An institution with a high credit risk will be more likely to default, resulting in a total loss for an investor.

Event Risk: a type of systematic risk associated with a securities price drop due to a major event. Whether an event risk can be helped or not, the end result may be the same. A high enough event risk can result in a substantial loss for an investor.

Failure Risk: Associated more with investing in startups, which is highly speculative because most startups will fail. Unlike an investment in a mature business with a mature model and reasonable growth expectations (where there is a track record success to analyze), there is a significant risk with developing and launching a new product into the market (which itself may be unproved). However, startup investing is often lucrative—and the majority of that style of investing is located in geographical pockets throughout the country but primarily located in the famed Silicon Valley (San Francisco).

Fraud: Inevitably, there will be certain nefarious individuals who are untruthful or outright fraudulent and have ulterior motives. If fraud or misleading conduct occurs, then the total investment may be lost, and that investment may or may not be recouped. Fraud is an intentional act and is not a mistake that happens. Fraud is when an investor is intentionally misled.

Industry Risk: a type of non-systematic risk associated with a particular type of industry, which is almost fully mitigated by investing across numerous companies and sectors.

Inflation Risk: a type of systematic risk associated with the bond market wherein the investment will not keep pace with or exceed inflation, which results in a partial loss to an investment potentially.

Interest Rate Risk: a type of systematic risk associated with changing interest rates and is relevant when trading in bonds.

Liquidity Risk: buying and securities are incredibly difficult. Startups are privately held, and there are no secondary markets available for private buyers to purchase securities. And there are often restrictions on the resale or transferability of securities. Liquidity risk is less common, however, with publicly held companies.

Non-Systematic Risk: these types of risks are broken into two major types—business risk and industry risk. Non-systematic risks can be almost fully mitigated, as discussed in this chapter.

Principal Risk: the potential of a total loss of one's investment, which can range from zero or close to zero to high.

For example, with the exception of equity crowdfunding, investing in startups is designed only for "accredited investors," precisely because the principal risk is so high with investing in pre-public startups, although the returns are almost always much higher in the event they do materialize.

Redemption Risk: the term has different uses in fiancé and business, but in terms of risk, it is a type of systematic risk and depends on how easy it is for an investor to get his or her money from an individual fund.

Reinvestment Risk: a type of systematic risk associated with reinvesting an interest or dividend payment, which is especially important when trading stocks and bonds that pay dividends with periodic interest.

Return Risk: There is no guarantee for specific returns on investment; in fact, ROI's can vary wildly and cannot be ensured. Some companies you invest in will no doubt become successful and generate large returns; many others will be unsuccessful, generate only a small return, or result in a loss.

Social Risk: A type of systematic risk wherein the risk is associated with social unrest and can cause a decline in the price of a particular security (if you're investing in overseas stocks, bonds, or currencies, for example, this is a common type of risk to become familiar with as social unrest is higher in certain countries versus others that are more stable).

Systematic Risk: this type of risk is associated with a particular investment, and there are many different types of systematic risks, including interest rate risk, credit risk, currency risk, and redemption risk.

Volatility Risk: a type of systematic risk that's associated with a security that may fluctuate more than expected due to some embedded problem inherent to the company.

OVERALL RISK CONCERN

You do not want to get too bogged down, at this time, in definitions, but those are some of the most common types of risk you should be concerned with, and going back over these and committing them to memory will be to be a sound strategy.

There are other types of risk, as well, but this book is not solely about risk, and despite even the types of risks we've discussed, none of them adequately address an individual investor's overall risk concern, unfortunately.

The more active an investor's strategy is, the more the investor must pay for exposure to that strategy. If he or she wants to have a lot of "skin in the game," for instance, and they have a pretty robust tolerance for risk, then they will typically have to pay a little bit more on the frontend.

On the backend, there's often more rewards associated with a more patient, low, and slow strategy. The key to getting rich—and retiring a millionaire—isn't to make a whole lot of money really fast, per se.

It's to invest wisely, be patient, and exercise good money management skills.

At the same time, we understand that every investment involves some varying amount of risk, which is close to zero for something like a government treasury to very high for something like investing in a startup, and that risk is quantifiable in absolute and relative terms, which is a major takeaway from this section.

Having a solid understanding of risk will no doubt help you as you manage your investment strategy, and between that and doing your proper due diligence, your assets will be much safer than taking a backseat approach to risk management and asset protection.

The fact is, if you have something worth protecting, you must actively protect it—and think about clever ways to do so. We recommend speaking with a trained professional if possible.

A BRIEF OVERVIEW OF ASSET PROTECTION

You may be asking, "Why am I worried about asset protection and risk management if I'm new to investing?"

You're right that maybe you do not have a lot of assets— for now. But that's at the heart of what we're trying to overcome, and in this section, we review asset protection principles, which will help you moving forward.

It's important to note that protecting your assets isn't about taking something that is due to the government, either. It's about protecting what you have as you make the right decisions moving forward. Simply put, it's about guarding one's wealth against outside forces that come in many forms.

We do not advocate not paying your taxes or doing anything else that's illegal, for that matter, but we do not want you overpaying either.

Asset protection is a crucial component of financial planning intended to protect a person's assets from unnecessary taxes, creditor claims, or anywhere else, and individuals (as well as companies) use asset protection to limit creditor's access or other unwarranted to access to valuable assets needed to grow.

Many states allow exemptions for a specified amount of home payments and other property—including personal clothing.

When we do not utilize those exemptions, we're literally giving the government money they do not require.

A company called SmartAsset is legally bound to act in your best interest—so I don't mind recommending them, at all, and if you'd like to be matched with a particular advisor, please reach out to me for further guidance or get started by following the linked address in this endnote.[y]

A properly established plan performs three very crucial functions which are lawsuit deterrence, settlement negotiation, and, or placing your assets out of the reach of a legal opponent; of course, you would hope to implement a proper asset protection strategy prior to planning a lawsuit or any cause of action, and if done so, it can be implemented anytime through rigorous planning.

Chapter 6

Where Do We Go from Here?

OVERVIEW

Claudia burst through the office door and seemed panicked. The entire office and everyone in it stopped moving—and watched as Claudia stomped toward Carson's backroom office.

She was visibly shaken and asked, "I'm sorry that I didn't make an appointment, but we had talked about doing so. It's just that I'm incredibly upset. Do you have time to meet with me today?"

"I do," he said, motioning with his hands. "Please, have a seat. I have all the time you need," he assured her, as they both took seats across from one another in the office.

Carson had some plaques, degrees, and certificates on the wall. Claudia examined the contents more closely than before. One degree was a Bachelor's in Accounting from USC, and another one was an MBA from UCLA.

"Did you go into debt getting those degrees?" Claudia said, before quickly backtracking. "I'm sorry. I think maybe that was kind of rude. I guess I'm just frustrated with college, work, and everything going on at home."

"It's perfectly understandable," Carson said. "But to answer your question, yes. I used to have a lot of financial problems, frankly. In fact, don't feel alone at all. Did you know that I once came into an adviser's office, myself and that I was sitting in your exact shoes, not knowing which way to turn?"

He paused then added, "Well, I guess it's actually been about twenty years by now, and wow, how time flies."

He started looking at the pictures on his desk and then picked up one, in particular, a 5 x 7 of a young man and a young woman and handed it to Claudia.

"I noticed that one before," she admitted. "Who are they?"

"That's me and my wife. She was my best friend," he continued, as his eyes started to mist. He caught himself and then quickly regained composure. "We were really close. We were completely inseparable from the point we met until—"

He paused, hesitating.

"I don't like to talk about it much, but let's just say that I'm accustomed to hard times myself, and that picture represents a time for me when I was happier than I'd ever been. Isn't that funny?" he asked. "You see, way back then, I was still working on my bachelor's degree and didn't have much money but was happy, nevertheless."

He looked around his office, nodding at the other degrees, certificates, signed autographs, and other memorabilia.

"I didn't have a pot to pee in as the old adage goes—but I had HER. We had each other, and we were as happy as two peas in a pod. Pardon the cliché."

"It's okay," she laughed. "I understand. My girlfriend and I are quite happy, but I think I'd be happier if I had more money."

"You would think so," he added. "But the secret to life isn't how many degrees you have, how many nice cars you drive, how much of the green stuff you have in your wallet. It can certainly help, but there's definitely more to life than money."

She was surprised to hear her financial advisor speak like this for the first time.

"What happened?" she asked.

"I really shouldn't be talking to you about this. It's not professional. I'm supposed to be helping you."

"No, it's ok. I want to know."

He paused, gathered his thoughts, and then continued.

"We would eventually get married. Like a lot of people, we couldn't afford to buy a home, so we rented. But we were happy in love with each other. I wasn't' making as much money back then, but it didn't matter to us. I never realized how happy I was then because I was so concerned with chasing money that I'd forgotten what life was all about before long."

"I think I understand what you mean."

"One thing I learned is that success depends on who's asking. It has to do with finding what you love—and being able to do that for a living and having loved ones who love you, as well. At least, that's what success means to me. I'd give all my money back if I could spend just one more day with my wife, for example."

"I'm so sorry for your loss," she said. "She was very pretty."

"She was very smart too. She went into STEM—despite her parents telling her that women aren't supposed to be interested in math and science. She was a brilliant engineer. Oh my goodness, she'd pour over her mathematics books for hours at a time."

"What happened to her?"

"She had cancer—and our insurance was capped. Our options were very limited at the time. We didn't have one of those fancy Cadillac insurance plans back then. And I didn't have the money to keep up with all the treatments."

"That's terrible."

"I don't know that she would have survived otherwise—but I would like to have given her a better chance. You know what I mean?"

"I'm so sorry to hear that. I'm sure you would have gone to the ends of the earth for her."

He nodded, still looking at that same 5 x 7 frame.

"It gets better with time, and as you can see," he added, looking up. "I really enjoy what I do, and that helps pass the time. I like working with young and up and coming individuals and helping steer them in the right direction and avoid many of my own pitfalls. One of those is thinking you have to be rich."

"But, you're a financial advisor?"

"I am. And I think people need to have clear-cut goals and plan accordingly. I think it's crucial. But everyone has a different definition of 'rich.'"

"You're not like any money manager I've ever met," she said. "In fact, I think you're the first money manager or adviser I've met—but you're certainly not what I expected."

"It's time to give back, Claudia! Take you. I don't want to see you strapped with more student loans than you can handle, making it nearly impossible to move away from home and eventually launch that business of yours."

"That's what I wanted to speak with you about. I've been thinking more and more about going to a larger university after community college. I'd like to have a degree to fall back on, whether I launch that business or not. But I'm scared to death about the student loan crisis."

"As well you should be," he replied. "I tell you what, let me buy you a cup of coffee, and you can tell me all about your girlfriend, your siblings, your family, and I'll tell you more about how to plan for college the smart way!"

"That sounds like a plan," she agreed. "Except the coffee's on me!" she insisted.

They got up and walked out of the office, which opened up to a sprawling outdoor shopping strip.

At the center of the strip was a large fountain. They agreed to grab a cup of coffee at the local coffee shop and then have a seat by the fountain and enjoy the warm California breeze and continue their conversation. Let's take a look at some of the topics they discussed.

THE STUDENT LOAN FIASCO

We covered some of the basic data associated with the student loan fiasco earlier, but we did not cover the very real implications that data has for individuals and families, many of whom are feeling broke, broken, with no real hope of finding a resolution. After doing so, we sill launch into a brief section on college planning—for those readers who are interested in means of funding their college without assuming much (if any) debt.

The real problem with the whole crisis is that there's not enough good education, information, or support in place to help families (and students) make smarter choices when it comes to college, particularly while they are still in high school—or earlier. Meanwhile, as the following chart indicates, the number of borrowers and the amount of debt is skyrocketing.[z]

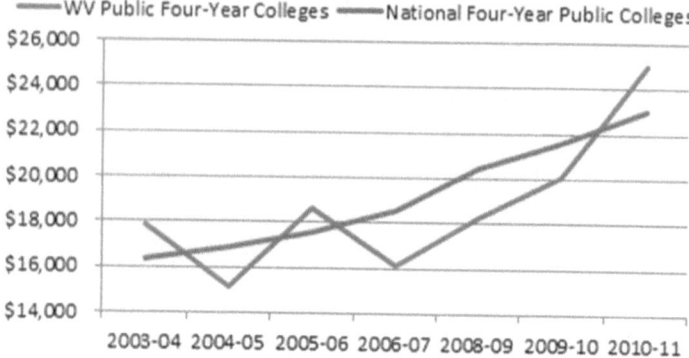

Average Debt of College Graduates

▬ WV Public Four-Year Colleges ▬ National Four-Year Public Colleges

Source: The Institute for College Access & Success, College Insight

Student loan debt was only about $500 billion collectively as of 2006, but there are now more than 40 million borrowers who actively owe about $1.5 trillion in loans. This, while the federal (and state) governments are spending billions of dollars on subsidies and regulations to attempt to curb alcohol use, tobacco and vape use, and drug prevention.

We decided that young folks shouldn't be able to access those things—because those things are bad for them, and we want them to make better decisions for themselves. This is particularly true, as of late, with vaping, which is now being linked to untold numbers of deaths in young people.

The science on vaping is still, unfortunately, unclear, but it's a safe assumption it's bad for you, and whether it's a safe alternative to cigarettes for adults is still in doubt.

Regardless, most people would agree with at least some of those regulations, whether you consider yourself a "leftist" or a "rightist." It just seems like the right thing to do. Young people should not be smoking and doing drugs, and most of us can all agree with that.

But at the same time, why do we enable students to take on debt they cannot afford to repay for degrees that will not yield them the kind of returns they hope for as wages continue to stagnate and the gap between males and females continues to divide us?

I say that because about 90% of private student loans, according to an article on CNBC's site, are signed by parents or other guardians, meaning they are enabling poor decisions in many cases.[aa]

We know better than to hand our children a cigarette or vape. We certainly would not hand an untrained child a loaded gun and tell them to go and play in the street or anywhere else, for that matter.

Yet, that's exactly what we're doing with student loan debt, a situation I knew all too close in my youth. Students are being enabled to make poor decisions while having not having access to alternatives. They are being given a loaded gun, frankly, which has tremendous negative implications on their futures.

CLAUDIA'S CASE STUDY

For a better look at the very real impact of the student loan crisis on individuals, let's use a hypothetical case study involving Claudia.

Claudia is a fairly common young lady. She works hard. She has a job as a hairdresser with dreams of owning her own salon (or salons) someday. She wants to also get a degree to "fall back on," and she's just now starting to think about investing, retirement planning, and budgeting, which actually puts her far ahead of the curve from a lot of millennials.

But unless Claudia plans accordingly, she might expect to take in about $40,000 (for easy math) to get her bachelor's degree, maybe more, maybe less. The average, by the way, is about $33,000.

She's going to school from 2019 until presumably about 2023, and the interest rates on her loans stand at about 6.8%. Without getting into cost-income calculations, let's say there's not much left over to move away from home, pay her own rent, utilities, transportation, and other living expenses.

On a 10-year repayment plan, Claudia will owe about $460 per month for something she does not physically own (it lives in her brain), and here's a short-list of things she cannot hope to do over that ten year period because of loan payments:

1. She cannot put $460 per month into a retirement plan.
2. She cannot save an extra $460 per month.
3. She cannot invest that $460.
4. She cannot buy a car with that $460.
5. She cannot purchase a wedding ring for her girlfriend for that $460 (if she plans on getting married). They cannot take a honeymoon, either, most likely.
6. She may not be able to account for medical bills— expected or otherwise—as was the case with her money manager and advisor, Carson, when he was younger.

What else can she NOT do because of that payment? And when I said $460, that assumes she makes on-time monthly payments totaling $5,520 per year for ten straight years (or 120 straight months).

That also doesn't assume she takes any penalties, rate hikes, or has anything else happen to unexpectedly throw her into default, which will hurt her credit rating and further affect her future potential. It's gone a dire picture.

But this case study was not meant to depress you, my dearest reader. It was meant to paint a sobering portrait of the realities of the student loan crisis, which seems to have an interesting relationship on home prices (according to the following chart).[bb]

The relationship between home prices and student loan default rates

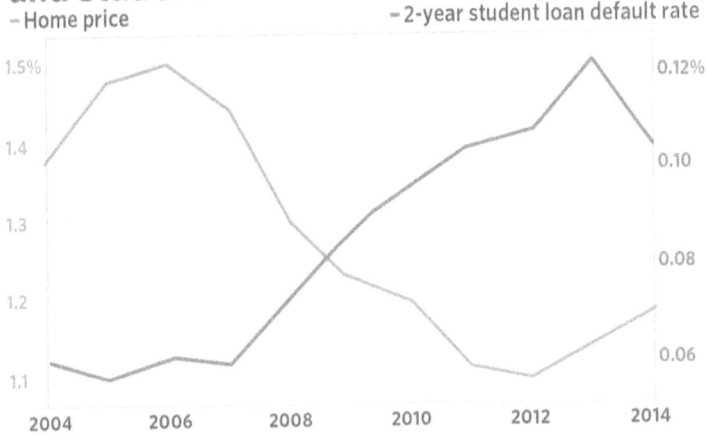

Sources: Zillow Home Value Index, National Student Loan Data System for Students

As we see, the lower defaults go, the lower home prices go—and vice versa. As you can see, the student loan fiasco is a problem in and of itself—even if you do not default. It reaches its tentacles into almost every part of society.

And, given our case study, what if she does default?

She would simply join one of the 11.4% of borrowers who are 90 or more days delinquent (and that doesn't count the ones who are in forbearance or deferment where you put your payments aside for a set amount of time while it continues to accrue interest.

According to Forbes, there are 44.7 million borrowers who account for $1.56 trillion in student loan debt, and the average class of borrowers leaves school with about $33,000 in debt, which is directly in-line with our case study.[cc]

According to that same source (based off 2018 numbers), certain states are hit the hardest by this crisis, namely California with $111.7 billion in student loan debt cumulatively with Texas following with $85.4 billion, New York with $73.5 billion, Florida with $72.8 billion, Georgia with $50.7 billion, Pennsylvania with $50.3 billion, Illinois with $49 billion, Ohio with $49 billion, Michigan with $40.8 billion, and North Carolina with $36.3 billion.

As you can see, the numbers are scary—and so too is Claudia's case study. But what if there was a better way? What if you didn't have to be broke and broken?

COLLEGE PLANNING

If you've already accumulated student loan debt—as I did—there is still hope for you. You most certainly do not have to remain broke and broken.

However, ideally, we would be budgeting and planning for college in advance and forego the realities of those other 45 million or so Americans. Let's review some ways to plan for college and avoid taking on all that debt in the first place.

The average cost of a public two-year college for in-district students is about $3,600. It's about $10,000 for a public four-year college for in-state students. It's about $26,000 for public four-year college for out-of-state students, and it's about $35,000 for a private four-year college according to numbers assembled via Dave Ramsey's blog.

I can safely say that student loan debt is a bad idea. Now, I get it. If there's no other option, if there's been thorough planning of your specific circumstances, I could perhaps understand if a person felt obliged to take out a small amount of fixed-interest, government-subsidized loans (wherever possible as with Stafford and other programs), but if at all possible, it should be avoided.

It also doesn't have to be borrow money—or skip going to college, either. But what if you want to be a doctor, a nurse, a lawyer, an engineer, or some other industry that requires a certain terminal degree for entry? Do you just find another option if you cannot afford college?

No. But if you plan ahead, you will find much more luck at leaving college without debt than otherwise. It happens all the time—believe it or not.

I suggest working with your parents or other guardians and start budging for your degree early in life—as in childhood (or at least by high school).

Think about all the costs involved from tuition to books to lodging to transportation to meal plans and more. Think about what degree you're going to pursue and know that in advance.

Understand the exact costs and start budgeting accordingly. We've already suggested numerous budgeting apps that will help you and/or your parents or guardians earmark certain savings for college.

If you're like many young Americans and you're facing the first day of college—and haven't managed to budget and save, yet, do not panic. While it's recommended to plan for college years in advance, there are other options, too, and if you take those opportunities and run with them and have already saved money, then hypothetically, that money can be changed from being earmarked for college to being earmarked for investment, retirement, buy a home, or some other goal.

College is expensive, so apply for all the aid you can and start with your **FREE APPLICATION FOR FEDERAL STUDENT AID or FAFSA**. These have to be filled out for each fiscal year, so make sure to update yours and refile each year. You will be assigned a pin. Keep track of that for your records, and you will be asked specific information concerning your college and type of degree being pursued and other personal information on a secured site. For access to that site, please refer to this endnote at your leisure.[dd]

The FAFSA is a form you or your loved one must complete each year. The types of aid it covers include federal grants, work-study, state aid, and various school aid dependent on the institution (you can list several schools on your FAFSA if you haven't settled on a school yet and those schools will be notified when you submit your application and start preparing a specific packet for financial aid options for you based off the information received).

Even if you have all the money you need in advance (which is exceedingly rare), everyone should fill-out a FAFSA form, because there is not an income cut-off to be eligible for financial aid, and you never know what you may qualify for until you try.

The FAFSA has a specific deadline, which can vary per state and per school, so refer to the site we noted in the aforementioned endnote and find out what the deadline for submission is for you and what information you need to fill it out (W-2s, 1040's, etc.).

Once you've submitted this form, you will receive an **EXPECTED FAMILY CONTRIBUTION** or **EFC** that estimates how much your family can expect to contribute toward your college. The specific college or university you choose will take that number into consideration.

In many cases, the EFC is ZERO, meaning there is no expected family contribution, so you can expect to receive more options for aid.

Of course, some of those options are loans—but other options include PELL GRANTS, other types of grants (these do not have to be repaid), work-study, and other options that do not have to be repaid.

It's possible, you won't have to pay anything if you get enough grants, and what little you do have to pay may offset by savings or working part-time at school.

Also, make sure to choose an affordable school. Think about your budget and how much the school costs (all associated costs) before making a decision.

There are a lot of factors that go into choosing the right school—so don't get blinded by fancy sports stadiums, brand recognition, or other less meaningful issues. The most important element for determining the right fit is easy. It's affordability. Do not let anyone tell you otherwise!

That doesn't mean your dream school is completely out of reach, but it does mean if you go to a more expensive school, you will need plenty of aid, preferably in the form of grants, scholarships, and work-study. You should be avoiding any kind of loans like the plague.

The goal here is simple—to show you that the most important thing is getting the degree you need while staying out of debt to hopefully forego the student loan crisis.

If that's the case with you, then this section is definitely for you.

As with Claudia, she chose to go to community college first before pursuing her bachelor's degree at a college or university if you recall from her example. The reason is that community college is much cheaper and often encompasses the same core requirements as large institutions.

If you have a potential issue with what may transfer and what will not, you can contact your school of choice and go over your transcript with them. Go to their main site and find the Registrar's Office or an intake academic advisor, find out who to speak with, and send them an email or phone call.

Sadly, a lot of people seem to think that going to a community college first will somehow hurt them later at a job interview with a future employer, and that's not the case under most scenarios. The important thing is not where you get your basic coursework done. It's where you got your degree from, what that degree was in, and how you performed while you were going there.

Trade schools are another option potentially—but it depends on what you plan on doing you're your degree and education, and you should not ignore the possibility of going to a trade school, especially when those schools offer practical skills that are great in areas like HVAC and electric.

Completing a trade school generally takes less time, as well. They are also cheaper and often include great job placement services that should be thoroughly examined prior to enrollment.

Take Claudia, for example. She may uncover that a four-year program—or community college—is not right for her, even though she's already started.

We will have to find out which choice she settles on, but let's not get ahead of ourselves.

We saved the best part for now, and that's to apply for scholarships. Now that we've had the basics of which schools are the most affordable and some options on paying for them without taking on debt let's think about scholarships, which can be a great way to fund your education, often with no out of cost expense for the student!

Firstly, start your scholarship search early. Don't wait until say July when you're going to enroll in August or September. Have that FAFSA filled out early and start your scholarship hunt much like you would any good job hunt.

I recommend that if you're already in high school, spend a few hours each week researching scholarship opportunities and finding and filling-out every single scholarship opportunity that you come across. In fact, we've even included a helpful link to help kick-start your scholarship search, but the onus is completely on you.

Do you want to graduate from college completely debt free? It's possible. Start with this endnote and find out how.[ee]

As with Fintech, the internet is going to be your best friend, and there are lots of options available today. Of course, you must be prepared to write some essays, which is why I said to set—at a minimum—a few hours aside each week doing your scholarship hunt.

You can also get in contact with various local community groups, businesses, and charities, which offer scholarships or grants—and some employers offer tuition reimbursement.

Grants mean they do not have to be paid back, and schools, the federal government, state governments, and various organizations are offering grants, which are typically tied to your financial need.

Once you've completed your FAFSA, you'll get information back on what federal grants you qualify for—but your hunt doesn't have to stop there. For more opportunities, check out this link (in our endnotes) via the US Department of Education, which will help you on your hunt for various state grant agencies.[ff]

You can work while you're in school, and believe me, from experience, it is possible. A lot of people think that working while in school is not a good idea and could interfere with performance, but I think the opposite is true.

You don't want to overwork yourself, but it's been my experience through research and things I've encountered along the way, that a certain amount of work while in school can actually be beneficial.

I recommend not working for more than 20 hours per week, and some of your options include work-study programs, off-campus jobs, and having a side hustle.

Side hustles are particularly popular these days, and as you might expect, we've included an entire section on some great ways to earn extra money, particularly if you're someone who's pursuing an education and looking for great ways to make extra cash, pay for that education, and in some cases, lead to greater opportunities later.

HOW TO START A BUSINESS OR SIDE HUSTLE

I know people who had so-called side hustles and ended up quitting their day jobs—so don't snub your nose at side hustles just yet. You might be surprised what all is available today, sometimes from your home, making studying when you're not working easier than ever.

First things first, you have to know what you're passionate about—and only you can answer that question. For example, Claudia is passionate about hairdressing and styling. So, that's why she works in a salon and is even contemplating launching her own business someday.

Still yet, for some people, a side hustle merely means signing up for a job at a restaurant and waiting tables or working at a retail store and selling candles or other products. I would not want to personally classify those as side hustles; those, in my opinion, are more traditional jobs. The fact is you don't have to just any job to add some money to your closely monitored account.

If you, for example, enjoy crafting, you can create an online store, make a Facebook and Instagram account, and start selling your products at local shops or markets. Or, let's say you're passionate about cooking, perhaps think about catering as a choice, although I must add that catering can be time-consuming, and if you're looking for more of a side hustle for now, perhaps try some of these other options.

After finding out what you're passionate about, figure out your schedule, and determine what kind of hours you're willing to work. We are talking a lot about college-age young men and women in this chapter, and with most of them, they may only need to work about twenty hours per week, so they have plenty of time to go to class, do homework, study, get rest, and other aspects of normal, everyday life.

Let's say you know you can manage a few evening shifts at a local café. You can earn $100 to $300 per shift waiting tables, and waiting tables is the preferred "side hustle" for a lot of young Americans.

I've even known professional servers who earn well in excess of $60,000 per year and do that for a living, and there's nothing wrong with that, either.

You should also network and find out what other people are interested in and find out if it's something you might like. Reach out to friends, loved ones, neighbors, people in your online community, other colleagues, and find out if anyone knows any great opportunities.

Let's say Individual A knows Individual B. They've been friends for years. Individual B is a college student, and he's looking to make some extra cash. He was able to get all the money he needed for tuition and dorm via grants and scholarships—but Individual B cannot eat tuition or mattresses. He needs food, oddly enough, and so he networked with Individual A, and as it occurred, that person is earning a nice living with a new side hustle of his own. Individual A is doing grocery deliveries for the popular platform Instacart and earning $1,000 per week or more on average, albeit full-time.

Individual A informed Individual B that you can take orders on-demand with Instacart and that he should try grocery deliveries in his area part-time to earn extra cash. Individual A informed Individual B that he's actually making over $25 per hour on average so that if he works hard too, Individual B can expect to earn about $500 per week in 20 or 25 hours. If that sounds too good to be true, it's not.

There are a lot of side hustles like Instacart, Amazon, Walmart, and other delivery companies that are paying people to do deliveries in their personal vehicles plus tips.

If delivering groceries—or packages for Amazon—isn't something you'd be interested in, perhaps you'd be interested in an entirely different hustle. Just keep in mind to keep your options open, network with peers, set financial goals for yourself, and figure out what you're passionate about.

The **GIG ECONOMY** is hot these days, and while often you do not get the traditional benefits of healthcare and retirement, doing side hustles can be a great way to earn extra income and get yourself through school debt-free.

Here are some good ideas to help kick-off your search for side hustles, those include e-commerce, caregiving, photography, dog walking, delivery, service industry, freelance editing or writing, and web design, to name a few.

As far as e-commerce, there's any number of things you might sell, and there are lots of places online that make that possible. We noted earlier that if you're crafty, there are plenty of options for you, and you might try using Etsy. Or, if you enjoy refurbing products, you might sell those products on various websites or create your own online store. As you can imagine, these kinds of jobs give you a whole lot of flexibility, as they're things you can mostly do from home.

Caregiving is another option for side hustles, especially if you have a knack for helping people; if so, you can do a little babysitting on the side, just as one example. There are options for taking care of the elderly during the day, but make sure to check online for what options might be available in your area.

Making the process easier, there are websites that enable you to launch your own business and help get you "gigs," which are official short-term jobs.

For example, the popular website known as care.com allows you to offer your nannying services specifically to people who are looking for that very thing.

If you're like a lot of people, though, you may actually prefer pets—to humans. If that's the case, you might want to try rover.com, which is similar to care.com but for pets. You create a profile on their account if accepted into its network.

People in need of doggy and other pet style daycare and lodging services can find you there, connect, and before you know it, you'll have your first job booked.

Of course, this is easier if you live off-campus—if you're a college-aged person.

Make sure your landlord is okay with housing pets, and if so, using Rover and other pet daycare platforms are an excellent way to earn money. You can earn in the neighborhood of $75 per night housing a pet (you can set your preferences for the type of pet) while you're doing another side hustle or studying.

Equally rewarding is the area of photography that has continued to soar in recent years. If you have a passion for taking pictures, why not put that to use for you and earn some extra cash? Consider photography for your side hustle and offer to take family portraits for people, engagements, or other events. We suggest doing a free webpage (with cheap domain hosting) to offer your services and linking your social media account. If you're looking for a good, free-to-cheap website builder that's copy-and-paste kind of simple, you may want to try wix.com or some other related service for your photography business—or other side hustle.

We noted delivery platforms like Instacart, and others already, so just make sure to apply in advance through their main site, find out where the services are being offered, and make sure your license, registration, and insurance are up to date. You can earn plenty of extra money grocery shopping and/or delivery groceries on a platform like Instacart or Shipt.

If you're already in school and you're good at writing or editing, you may consider doing some freelance ghostwriting or editing on a platform like Fiverr or Upwork. With both platforms, you have to create a profile that showcases your abilities. Just be careful not to overpromise and underdeliver. Know what you're good at—and the chances are, it's something you can make money at like ghostwriting, editing, cover art, blogging, or web design.

The main difference between Upwork and Fiverr are in how you procure jobs. On Upwork, you bid for jobs that buyers place, whereas, on Fiverr, freelancers offer their services to the public via their platform, and buyers have the opportunity to approach them.

It's a great way to earn a little extra cash—and if you're particularly good at it, there are articles on Forbes and elsewhere that indicate some sellers are making comfortable six-digit salaries on Fiverr and have abandoned their corporate careers altogether.

More people than ever are forgoing full-time, traditional employment for so-called side hustles, and as we've demonstrated, there's a lot of options to choose from.

Side hustles offer the kind of flexibility that's practically unparalleled in the "real world," and those positions range from things as simple as moonlighting at a bar or restaurant to walking or babysitting dogs or other pets on the side to delivering groceries to freelancing and many more.

Lastly, don't think because you thought about one career option for a while or went down a certain road for months or years, that it's too late to make a full pivot into something else.

Just remember, if you're already working, it's always best to put in a notice, but go out there and find something you are passionate about.

From my experience, most people who feel broke and broken, are in a job they despise—and I want so much more for each of my followers and readers.

There are inevitably a lot of ups and downs, and everyone's circumstances are different, but as this chapter indicates, there are also a number of great ways to get through college debt-free and discover a passion for something you can actually make money at. For you, that might just mean launching your own business from home and earning money that way!

As you're looking ahead at the next few years of your life, just keep some of those things in mind, and before we wrap things up, we'd also like to discuss making the first big move away from your parent's home.

MOVING AWAY FROM HOME

It's no doubt that many of my readers are still living at home with their parents, which is no surprise if you think about the looming student loan crisis, stagnant wage growth, and hyperinflating college costs, health care costs, and other inflation.

As far as Claudia, we know that she also lives at home with her family—who wholly support her in everything that she does.

In fact, in many ways, her parents would just assume her live with them forever, because they love her and want to protect her. Not to mention, there's the whole issue with the soaring cost of housing, whether you choose to buy—or rent.

At the same time, Claudia is ready to spread her wings—and fly out of the coupe altogether, and we wanted to give her and our readers some tips on moving away from their parents' homes for the first time.

While living at home, Claudia has had the financial safety net that comes from her parents. Her parents are immigrants who work hard to provide for their family, and that comfortability that comes from that can be hard to want to voluntarily forego.

But if you're going to move away from her, firstly, do it for the right reason. There's no rule that says if you're 18—or even say 21 to 25—that you "have" to move away from home at a certain point.

At the same time, it's easy to get complacent and not want to change. So, make sure you're doing it for the right reason.

If you find out, after some careful soul searching, that moving away from home is right for you, then please consider the following tips. These suggestions should not be taken for specific advice, however, because, in some cases, it might be best for you to continue living at home while pursuing your degree or trade school.

If you do move out, start planning months and months in advance and make sure to track your monthly income, preferably using one of the apps we suggested earlier.

Start by listing things that are considered **NON-NEGOTIABLE PAYMENTS**, meaning things that have to get paid like groceries, rent or mortgage, phone, utilities, and so on.

Figure out from there exactly how much income you will need and how much you can afford for rent/mortgage. There are also costs associated with moving, so plan your budget for actually moving out—including the costs of a moving company (if necessary, but we suggest involving as many "free" friends and family as possible).

If you have to hire a moving company or rent a moving van, check out prices in advance before choosing the one that's the most affordable. And if you don't need a really large U-Haul, you may be able to get away with something that's smaller—and thusly, more affordable.

Determine what you have left for other purchases once you've done that because you will need money for a deposit and other first-time expenses. You should start having a pretty good idea at this point what it's going to cost you to actually move out.

Assuming you already have gainful employment (or lucrative side hustle), find a suitable place that's right for you and your budget. One option might be a small, inexpensive apartment for your first place away from home.

If you're moving because of school, check the local options available online, and some schools will help you find accommodations for living on or off-campus, as well. The main thing is to stick to your budget and don't overextend.

You know how much you make, how much you have saved (and for what) versus what it's going to cost to move, sustain yourself once you're there, and make those recurring non-negotiable payments for several months while you get your feet established underneath you in your new environment.

We also suggest practicing some good habits before you move away from home, and the whole idea behind that is because when we live with our parents or other loved ones, it's easy to get really comfortable and to forget all the hard work that goes into upkeeping your own home.

You have to do more than make your own bed, for example, so we suggest to start thinking and acting more like a mature, grown-up in this regard—and start practicing for when you have your own place.

You may decide to get a place with a friend or rent a room from someone that's close to your new school or job. If that's the case, be very careful who you invite into your house and vet everyone accordingly.

It's not a stalker. It's called being proactive and mature and planning properly. Also, don't be afraid to ask your parents (or guardians) for help. I mean—seriously, that's what they're there for.

Plus, you know they've likely done all this stuff before, and they can help you to understand what to expect. If you need help laying out those expenses in advance, they can likely help there, too, and as always, we want to fully encourage you to budget and use one of the budgeting apps to make the process easier.

Your parents will be going through their own emotional roller coaster if you're leaving for the first time—but I can almost guarantee you that they're willing to support you, especially since you're about to embark on a whole new journey in life.

On a few housekeeping notes, also remember to pack smart in advance and try to consolidate your belongings, which will save you time and money on your move. There's a lot of things to plan for, though, and we've only covered the basics, so as we wind this section down, we want to remind you that its always a good idea to create a list.

When you create a list, you will be able to see everything that needs to be done from changing your address at the post office, having utilities turned on, paying any deposits necessary, and buying essentials for your house (don't go crazy and realize that some purchases can be spread out as you start to slowly accumulate everything you need).

Remember that we only recommend hiring movers if it's absolutely necessary to save money. The chances are, if you ask nicely, there are a few people in your life who would be willing to help for free or very cheap.

If you do have to hire a van or truck (or a moving company), always do your homework and find the right deals for your budget.

If you're not sure about which is better between buying or renting, we advise not to make any drastic decisions early in life. There's actually plenty of pros associated with both options, but one thing about buying means that you're likely to be stuck in a particular location for longer than you may realize.

As a young person, in this author's opinion, the decision to buy a house—and the debt and costs that entails—should not be taken lightly, and sometimes, it's actually better to rent versus buy and keep your flexibility open so that you can move as necessary for your budding career.

Unfortunately, we also know that not everything involving being broke and broken can be fixed with a new app—or a helpful tip or "hack." The mindset of being broke often permeates whole families and can have generational side effects for many years to come.

But does it have to be that way? Are there solutions to this most-pressing issue?

THE PSYCHOLOGY OF BROKE, BROKEN

As people in the middle-class strive to be rich and live out the American Dream, the gap between the rich and poor continues to grow, leaving some amongst us hopeless and heartbroken—or what we've simply called broke and broken.

Poverty is a psychological issue more than anything else, and while we wanted to put some tools and concepts into your vocabulary that will no doubt help your financial wellbeing, we also wanted to briefly address the psychology of being poor and offer suggestions how to move forward.

If you're like Claudia or any number of other poor or middle-class people, you're often faced with the realities of financial scarcity and not knowing how the next month's rent payment or grocery bill will be met.

For these very obvious reasons, the biggest difference between the thought flows of the rich versus the poor or middle-class is in their conception of sufficiency.

A rich person thinks about how to spend money properly and how to make more of it, while a poor man thinks about how to find free time and earn money, as his assets are much scarcer.

But what if we put each of them in a separate room and gave them $10,000 apiece. Would the thoughts change? These are very interesting questions, no doubt.

In my opinion, the rich man would be more likely to think about how to take that $10,000 and make more of it, while the other man will think about how to find more money or spend what he has just been given.

These are two very different thought processes.

In other words, the poor man is the one who doesn't know how to use the opportunity given to him whereas the rich person, more used to these opportunities and less affected by the demands of scarcity, knows just how to deal with his newfound money.

One reason for this might be the poor man wasn't as used to having those opportunities—for whatever reason, but the purpose of our book is to address the "why" and move into the "how."

Namely, the idea was to take the tools that typically only the wealthy employ and put them into the hands of regular, everyday people like you and me.

The rich person will take it and wield it and make the best of the opportunity that's been presented to him; but, some people, inevitably, will not do that, and the differences are all in the flow of thoughts between how the rich think about money versus how the poor and middle-class think about money.

This also naturally assumes that everyone's given the same opportunities before that one-time payment. Or does it? While most of our behaviors are no doubt conditioned through a series of actions and reactions over many years, those conditioned responses can be altered with proper external stimuli (i.e., as with this book) and the person taking it and doing the right thing with it (i.e., as with putting it to work in your life).

Honestly, I cannot do that for you—or I would. In fact, I would be glad to do that for you.

But since I cannot, I've done the next best thing which is placed in your hands many of the tools you will need to start planning for your retirement, saving, and budgeting.

You may have to start small, but there's a profound effect on your whole psychology once you start seeing the results, which will come in short order. It won't happen overnight—but relish in your newfound success, even if its meager at first.

If it helps, you may also choose to reach out to me, join my network, and/or network with other followers in my circle.

Find other people, frankly, who are as positively hell bound on success as you are. I would even posit that you don't have to know exactly what tomorrow holds in order to start moving in the right direction today.

None of us are soothsayers, and those fortune cookies seldom lend good, tangible advice.

Focus on those small successes along the way and start shifting your thinking from what I have or don't have—to what I need and how I'm going to get! And that, my friend, is the key to unlocking your truest potential.

Claudia has learned a number of valuable lessons along the way, as well, and its certainly true that Carson is probably not quite like any financial advisor or money manager you've ever encountered, but that's because he's fictional.

He was just one of many tools to get you thinking and acting like a rich person, as you start to shift from broke and broken to successful and savvy.

The realities of scarcity will not evaporate overnight, but I can guarantee you that just by placing one foot in front of the other and heading in the right direction, you'll start feeling better before you know it.

Let's take a look at Claudia's situation once more and see what happens next.

WHAT HAPPENS NEXT FOR CLAUDIA?

The large, multi-tiered water fountain jutted up ten feet into the air from the center of a shallow pool of water that was about twenty feet in diameter and littered with years and years of people's wishes in the form of pennies, dimes, and nickels.

They had lost track of time in rapt conversation, and the bustling strip mall was starting to slow down with pedestrian foot traffic. The sun had not yet set and was casting a beautiful orange, blue glow as far as one could see.

They had talked about college planning, budgeting, and potentially moving away from home before a new thought occurred to Claudia.

"The more you tell me about trade school, the more interested I get."

"Is that right?" he replied. "You know, my intentions as far as that was to give you some pointers on getting your education without going into debt. But I didn't mean to suggest one option over another."

"I understand that, and I respect that, too. But the more I think about it, the more it makes sense. I mean, my whole life people were saying, college, college, college. You have to get a degree."

"Yea, that's pretty much been the mantra for decades now. But some areas require degrees, whereas many others do not."

"That's exactly my point. I don't need a business degree—or $40,000 in debt or whatever it would come to—if I'm already passionate about what I'm doing, and it doesn't require a degree."

"I think you're onto something with that, my friend. The only thing I've tried to do throughout our meetings is get you understanding your various options and encourage you toward tools that might make that easier. If college isn't the right path for you, it's just not. Trust me," he added. "Having a degree isn't some big-ticket toward instant happiness—or success."

"I think you're absolutely right. I had also been planning on moving away from home, but I'm starting to re-think that, as well. I just don't know that it would be the right move for me right now. I mean, my parents love me. I'm comfortable. I would miss my siblings dearly. And I can always move away from home once I'm more secure."

"That's exactly right, Claudia, and it's as we've discussed, the very biggest advantage that you have over say someone like ME," he said, perking up a bit. "Is that you are young. You have plenty of time on your hands."

"I'm going to start looking into local trade schools and find out if I can get a certificate or degree in cosmetology and see if that makes more sense for me."

"I think it's a fantastic idea. But again, I never planned on steering you one way or the other, especially with your college choice, but I did want to demonstrate that there are some less traditional ways that people are handling that part of their lives that don't include amassing mountains of debt," he added, looking up at the fountain.

He continued, "It's like that fountain. It's multi-tiered. There are three levels. The bottom level, the foundation, is the biggest. The middle tier is moderately large, then on up to the top where it's quite small."

"What are you getting at?" she laughed, her eyebrows curling up in the universal sign of confusion.

"You have to have the proper foundation before you can start to access all the things you want to come through in life. Think about it like the water that's falling out of each tier. The largest basin can hold the most—and it ought to. That's your college choices, our basic investment strategies, etcetera," he added. "Then, as we move up, things get smaller. There's less room in the basin, so fill it with things that you've built upon from the bottom level. That might be the car you're planning on buying you were telling me about."

"The one I said I was going to take out a high-interest loan on?"

"That's the one. So, we don't have room for that high-interest loan in our middle basin. But, if you save, if you make the investments, I will suggest, then you will have more money soon, and you can put as nice a car or nicer in there soon, and you won't have all that debt."

"That makes sense."

"I think so too," he quipped. "I just kind of made it up right here on the spot, so let's see how far I can take this metaphor. The top layer, now that's your goals and dreams, the big ones, that are way up at the top. There's not much room in that basin, and the water is spilling out much quicker. So, that's where your dreams go. Don't put too much in there at all or it gets all cluttered up and falls out anyway," he said, and with that, they both started cracking up.

"So, you're saying I'm pretty much like that big fountain then, huh?" she laughed. "With the water flowing out?"

"Yea. It's maybe not the best metaphor ever. But if you look closer," he added, as he stood up and motioned with his hand toward the middle basin. "You see all those coins in there?"

She nodded.

"That's all the stuff you can put in your fountain. And the one at the top that's up over my head," he said, laughing. "Well, it's so high I can't see in it, but if I imagined hard enough, I bet some folks have thrown a few of their dreams in there, too, but just keep in mind, there's not as much room at the top!"

"Hey, that actually is a great metaphor, Carson! I knew I liked you. You're not just a smart money guy, but you're pretty creative, too," she added, placing her empty coffee cup on the ledge.

She reached into her pocket and grabbed a few coins. She looked into her hands and had a few pennies, a quarter, and two nickels.

"Time to make a wish, Claudia," he said.

"Yes, it is," he replied and flicked the quarter up and over into the highest basin.

"What'd you wish?" Carson asked.

"Now, you know I can't tell you that! But thank you for all your advice. Time to start using it. I'm tired of feeling broke and broken."

Chapter 7
Closing Thoughts

Throughout this book, we've been reminded of the startling differences between the rich and the middle-class, and our goal was never to demonize the wealthy. The idea was to increase the amount of information available to our readers about wealth management, retirement, and budgeting and begin to familiarize them with specific tools they could actually access, many of which we also provided direct links to in our endnotes.

We covered a lot of data along the way, and that data is quite telling, namely the differences in the wage gap, the student loan fiasco, and more.

But we are not numbers. We are real, live people. For example, if you prick me—I assure you, I will bleed. I might even put up a fight—or run as my natural instincts kick-in.

Along the way, we've been introduced to a fictional character named Claudia. We learned about her, her family, her struggles, and her hopes and dreams. We also met a financial advisor, Carson.

We discussed how to plan for college—or trade school— without taking on enormous piles of debt. We also discussed side hustles and finding something you're passionate about and many more details.

While, in some ways, our fictional advisor may not be like most money managers, he was used (like Claudia) to help bring the realities of the serious issues we are dealing with into context and portray how those issues play out in the real world.

It's easy to stare at numbers or discuss topics or even discuss financial technology and other great tips, but I felt like when you see it for yourself that it might touch closer to home.

While this was also a sobering portrait of the realities of the middle-class, I promised you that there was a proverbial pot of gold at the end of the rainbow. If you're like I was or you're like our fictional friend, you may have to work ten times harder than others to succeed because you might not have been born with as much money as others.

But rest assured, when you do succeed, you will feel a gazillion times better off because no one earned it but you (with a little encouragement along the way).

It was always my sincerest goal that you would heed my words, learn from my story, and discover all the hidden gems of modern investing and money management information that's currently available.

Throughout my time at Merrill and Morgan, I met a shocking number of people who earned a typical middle-class income and were still able to retire millionaires. It wasn't easy.

However, it's also not only about how much money you make or even how you invest it. It's also about how you manage the money you do have and the whole way you think about money.

Briefly recall the section on psychology and poverty. We discussed that broke and broken is a mindset more than just a financial state. We noted how we could give $10,000 to two different people and have two very different outcomes.

One person was already rich, and the second person was "poor." The rich person took the ten grand and started quickly envisioning ways to make more money, while the poor person took the money and started thinking about how he might find more of it or where he could spend it.

That doesn't mean it was a perfect test study. We do acknowledge that the unique backgrounds of each person were different, but so to was the way they responded when given the same opportunity.

That's what I'd like to do with you today. No, it's not a check for $10,000, and I wish I could afford to give each of my readers (and social media followers) a kick-start in the right direction with a pile of cash, but I am giving you an opportunity, nonetheless.

You do not have to be broke and broken for much longer.

You can start changing your mindset right now—as you start to slowly implement the aforementioned tips and techniques.

I think, before long, you'll start to see a difference, and it will start with your own mind and the whole way you think about money and what it even means to be "rich."

Some people call the power of positive thinking guru-gibberish, but it's nothing of the sort at all. The positive energy you put out there will be attracted back to you.

You can transition your mindset from being broke and broken to being savvy and successful, and it won't take as long as you might imagine. The tools once only available to wealthy trust fund babies are increasingly more available to each and every one of us.

Regardless of which ones you use, however, it will start with your mindset. If you're feeling broke and broken, I'm here to say there's a better way.

I hope this book helps—but as always, if there's any way I can assist you further, please never hesitate to ask.

And if you need additional info, please refer at your leisure to the following glossary, references, and additional resources, or reach out to me on Instagram (@pedromfrias) or elsewhere.

Appendix A:
Investment Terms & Concepts

401(k): in the US, a 401(k) is a plan that is tax-qualified, defined-contribution based that individuals receive through their employers along with matching contributions.

Accredited Investor: In the USA, an accredited investor must have a net worth exceeding $1 million individually or with a spouse (excluding the value of the primary residence) or have earned income exceeding $200,000 ($300,000 if combined with a spouse) during each of the last two calendar years while demonstrating that income is a stable and securable source of income. Basically, an accredited investor means "millionaire." With the exception of EC, traditional securities sold by startups are only available to accredited investors because of government regulations.

Annualized Expenses: when creating a budget, it is highly recommended to also annualize your expenses as one part of that process in order to see the true costs involved in any major or presumably minor expenses.

Annuity: a fixed sum of money paid to someone over a period of time; it's also an insurance product that promises to pay regular income over time instead of more immediately. Annuities can be fixed or variable, and you can buy one with a lump sum of money or through a series of payments; this is taxed income and not taxed at capital gains rates.

APY or Annual Percentage Yield: a tool used by investors to deduce how much money they're earning, compared to a simple interest quote, the APY is considered a more accurate reflection of true earning potential and takes compound interest into account.

BLOCKCHAIN: a system in which a record of transactions is made in a cryptocurrency that is maintained across a series of computers that are linked together in a peer-to-peer network.

Bonds: This term means something issued by a company promising to repay borrowed money with certain conditions. It's basically a loan. A convertible bond (aka. convertible note and convertible debt) is a bond that also has the option of not repaying the borrowed amount in cash but in terms of equity. Convertible bonds are by far the most popular type of traditional securities for early-stage startups.

Business Risk: a type of non-systematic risk associated with investing in a particular company. Needless to say, business risks can come in many forms, namely company debt and other issues common to specific companies. This type of risk is easily mitigated by diversifying in various types of companies—and industries.

Capital Gains: a profit from the sale of a property or an investment that is taxed at a different rate than earned income.

Certificates of Deposit or CDs: a type of savings account with a fixed rate and a set maturity date. CDs typically do not have monthly fees and draw a small amount of interest.

Commissions: this type of performance-based compensation is traditionally based on the value of items sold. Commonly you see this as a form of payment for salespeople where they earn a percentage of the price at which the product or service was sold. In the startup world, offering commission-only compensation is a great way to attract people that care about your product or service and will invest in working with you for no compensation unless they bring in money. In the investor world, it just replies to the amount of money a manager charges for buying and selling securities on behalf of a client.

Credit Risk: a type of systematic risk associated with the overall creditworthiness of the company issue a particular bond. US-backed bonds, for example, have low to zero credit risk. An institution with high credit risk will be more likely to default, resulting in a total loss for an investor.

Default: when a bond issuer is unable to repay his debt, which results in lower credit rating (or other penalties) for the issuer, and, in some cases, a total principal loss for the investor. In terms of the student loan crisis, this term simply refers to borrowers who are 90-plus days delinquent and not in an approved forbearance or deferment).

Dividends: the distribution of a reward from a portion of a company's earnings, which are paid to shareholders.

Dow or Dow Jones Industrial Average: an index that tracks the thirty largest publicly-owned companies trading on the NYSE and the NASDAQ with major names like Apple and Disney.

Due Diligence: a phrase with different meanings dependent on the circumstance, but in investing, due diligence is an important aspect where an investor takes certain precautions before buying or selling something to safeguard themselves against potential loss.

Estimated Family Contribution or EFC: when you fill out your FAFSA, it will estimate how much your family can expect to contribute toward your college (beginning with zero).

Event Risk: a type of systematic risk associated with a securities price drop due to a major event (if you recall the Peloton add with the massive backlash in November 2019, I consider that a type of event risk, although most of the time event risks are associated with natural disasters and other major events, some of which cannot be helped). Whether an event risk can be helped or not, the end result may be the same. A high enough event risk, for example, can result in substantial losses for an investor.

Exchange-traded fund or ETF: a collection of (generally) thousands of individual units of stocks and bonds that are sold as funds within an exchange and are tracked on an index such as a stock index or bond index.

Extended Security: Unlike traditional securities, an extended security isn't governed by laws that came effect in the 1930s. Instead of representing ownership in the company itself, extended securities generally represent ownership over what the company produces from which the investor hopes to gain profit when/in the event the company does well. Like a traditional security, it is a structured promise of providing a return (financial or otherwise) when a company does well in the future. This can be represented as dozens of commonly used things including the many types of loans, revenue sharing agreements, the licensing of IP, or even the promise to use a particular firm in the future if that firm provides services upfront while deferring or reducing its fees until your startup meets some milestone. One common type of "extended security" is the pre-order customer (or "backer" on Kickstarter).

Failure Risk: Associated more with investing in startups, which is highly speculative because most startups will fail. Unlike an investment in a mature business with a mature model and reasonable growth expectations (where there is a track record success), there is a significant risk with developing and launching a new product into the market (which itself may be unproved).

FAFSA or Federal Application for Federal Student Aid: a form completed by current or prospective college students (undergraduate and graduate) in the US to determine their eligibility for student aid.

FICO Score: this term refers to a person's credit score, which is calculated via software from the Fair Isaac Corporation (FICO).

Founder Stock: founder stock is a subset of stock given to early founders and is issued at par value (approximately $0.0001 per share), and generally comes with a vesting (or reverse-vesting) schedule. According to the SEC, this stock is designed to be issued to those who "take the initiative in founding or organizing a business."

Fraud: Inevitably, there will be certain nefarious individuals who are untruthful or outright fraudulent and have ulterior motives. If fraud or misleading conduct occurs, then the total investment may be lost. Fraud is an intentional act. Fraud is not a mistake that happens to prove costly. Fraud is when an investor is intentionally misled. Many of these scenarios were discussed in the bagging of the last chapter.

Gig Economy: a labor market characterized by the prevalence of short-term contracts, agreements, or freelance work as opposed to a traditional and/or permanent job.

Hybrid Security: Any combination of multiple traditional or extended securities being bundled into one deal. For example, if you have watched Shark Tank, Kevin O'Leary likes to make an offer along these lines "I will give you $500,000 in exchange for 30% of your company AND $2 from every sale you make." When Kevin makes these offers, he is trying to buy a "hybrid security," which is made up of stock (a traditional security) and revenue sharing (an extended security).

Initial Public Offering or IPO: startups can only sell securities to "accredited investors," per SEC guidelines, but when a company moves into the public sphere, they can start selling their securities (such as common stock) on a stock exchange, beginning with an IPO.

Industry Risk: a type of non-systematic risk that's associated with a particular type of industry, which is almost fully mitigated by investing across numerous companies and sectors.

Inflation Risk: a type of systematic risk associated with the bond market wherein the investment will not keep pace with or exceed inflation, which results in a partial loss to an investment potentially.

Interest Rate Risk: a type of systematic risk associated with changing interest rates and is relevant when trading in bonds.

IRA or Individualized Retirement Account: there are different types of IRAs (such as Roth IRAs), but generally, they are individual retirement accounts with certain tax-advantages that investors or individuals can use to earmark funds for retirement.

Liquidity Risk: buying and securities are incredibly difficult. Startups are privately held, and there are no secondary markets available for private buyers to purchase securities. And there are often restrictions on the resale or transferability of securities. Up until recent years, there were also SEC guidelines, which restricted startup investment to accredited investors only, due, in part, to the lack of liquidity inherent to startup investing and a high potential for a total loss.

Margin Trading: a method of trading assets using funds provided by a third party, which tends to allow investors to access greater sums of capital versus regular trading accounts, allowing them to leverage their position.

Market Capitalization or Market Cap: one of the measures of determining a company's size and is based on the total market value of a company's outstanding stock (that investors own).

Market Index: a hypothetical portfolio of investment holdings that represent a segment of a financial market; the calculation of the index comes from the prices of the underlying holdings, and some indices have values based on market-cap weighting (the value of a company), revenue-weighting, float-weighting- and fundamental-weighting.

Maturity: generally refers to the preset timeline when a bond matures and the original principal of the bond is due plus any remaining interest, except in the unusual circumstance that the bond issue defaults (where the bond issuer is unable to repay the debt).

Mutual Fund: an investment program funded by various shareholders which trade in a mixture of holdings that are professionally managed; they are considered safer investments, on average, than individual stocks or bonds which have higher risk profiles due to associated company or industry risk variables.

NASDAQ: an electronic exchange where stocks are traded electronically instead of on a floor—as with the NYSE in former years.

Net Asset Value, NAV, or NAVPS: derived by dividing the total value of the securities in a portfolio by the total amount of shares outstanding (outstanding shares are held by individual investors, institutional investors, etc.).

New York Stock Exchange or NYSE: one of several major exchanges for buying and selling securities in the United States. Other countries have their own forms of exchanges similar in nature to the NYSE. Trading is now done electronically on the NYSE, and in recent years, there are far fewer people trading from the floor of the NYSE than there used to be when it was more paper-based.

Non-Negotiable Payments: when budgeting, it's important to know which payments or expenses are negotiable and which ones are non-negotiable (like rent, utilities, etc.).

Non-Systematic Risk: industry or company-specific risk inherent to most investments but that can be marginalized if not zeroed out through diversification in numerous companies and/or industries unlike its close relative, systematic risk.

Options: These are things like "SAFE notes" and employee options. These are a promise to sell someone equity in a company at a discount when certain milestones are met. A "warrant" is another similar instrument but, in many ways, more advantageous to the startup founder and the investor.

Primary Market: allows companies to issue and sell their equity via shares to the common public at-large through a process of initial public offerings or IPO's.

Principal Risk: the potential of a total loss of one's investment, which can range from zero or close to zero to high. For example, with the exception of equity crowdfunding, investing in startups is designed only for "accredited investors," precisely because the principal risk is so high with investing in pre-public startups, although the returns are almost always much higher in the event they materialize.

REIT or Real Estate Investment Trust: these can be traded on popular apps like Robinhood and are companies that own and/or operate income-producing real estate.

Redemption Risk: the term has different uses in fiancé and business, but in terms of risk, it is a type of systematic risk and depends on how easy it is for an investor to get his or her money from an individual fund.

Reinvestment Risk: a type of systematic risk associated with reinvesting an interest or dividend payment, which is especially important when trading stocks and bonds that pay dividends with periodic interest.

Return Risk: There is no guarantee for specific returns on investment; in fact, ROI's can vary wildly and cannot be ensured. Some companies you invest in will no doubt become successful and generate large returns; many others, on the other hand, will be unsuccessful, generate only a small return, or result in a total loss (to the investor).

Secondary Market: where investors buy and sell securities they already own.

Security: As defined in the Securities and Exchange Act of 1934 a traditional security, within the context of a startup or company, represents a percent of company ownership (via stock), a loan to the company (via bond), or the right to own a part of a company in the future (via options or warrants). A traditional security is something an investor buys from a company for money, and it represents ownership of the company, creditor, or rights to ownership on which the investor hopes to gain profit when/in the event the company does well.

By law, buyers of traditional securities need to be accredited, investors—as it pertains to pre-public startups. Further, some types of companies are not allowed to have or sell traditional securities at all (i.e., nonprofits).

Social Security Administration or SSA: the program that disburses benefits in the form of Supplemental Security Income (SS) and SSA benefits that was designed originally to help the disabled and retirees to supplement their income; however, in recent years, SSI and SSA benefits are being more heavily relied upon, in general, in recent years.

Social Security Benefits: the benefits received from the Social Security Administration (SSA) that are being relied upon more and more by retirees to make ends meet. These benefits were paid into by the recipient through a payroll deduction.

Social Risk: A type of systematic risk wherein the risk is associated with social unrest and can cause a decline in the price of a particular security (if you're investing in oversees stocks, bonds, or currencies, for example, this is a common type of risk to become familiar with).

Stock: there are two basic types of stock - Common stock or preferred stock (also called "shares"), which represent an equity stake in a company. All companies have different amounts of shares, yet every company needs to own 100% at all times. For example, one company may be valued at $100 and have one hundred shares—making each share worth $1. Another company may be valued at $100 but only have 10 shares—making each share worth 10% of the company. Percent of the company is what the Sharks in the Tank buy from founders.

Systematic Risk: an area of risk that encompasses several areas of risk and refers to the vulnerability to events of a certain company. There are a number of types of systematic risks to be cognizant of, some of which were discussed herein.

Tax-Sheltered Accounts: retirement accounts that are tax-deferred and act as a shelter in this manner from a larger tax burden those same dollars might see otherwise; for example, when you contribute to a 401(k), your taxable income decreases by the amount of that contribution.

Taxable Earned Income: refers to the amount of money that is subject to taxes after reducing your gross income by the value of your deductions and exemptions.

Value Proposition or Value Prop: the tangible value that a company brings to the market; in terms of Fintech, which is changing everything, much of the value prop is in the ease of access to new tools for investing, trading, and managing money, making the whole way average consumers access these tools more accessible than ever before.

Volatility Risk: a type of systematic risk wherein the risk is associated with a security that may fluctuate more than expected due to some embedded problem inherent with the company.

Voting Rights: certain shareholders have voting rights on the board of companies, which gives those shareholders some level of say (proportional to their shares) over a company's operations.

Appendix B:

Endnotes

---

[a] https://smartasset.com/retirement/the-average-salary-by-age

[b] https://www.payscale.com/data/gender-pay-gap#section02

[c] https://www.payscale.com/data/gender-pay-gap

[d] https://www.latinousa.org/2018/10/30/latinawagegap/

[e] https://www.payscale.com/data/gender-pay-gap#section03

[f] https://www.forbes.com/sites/zackfriedman/2019/02/25/student-loan-debt-statistics-2019/#2e18e226133f

[g] https://markets.businessinsider.com/news/stocks/wall-street-charging-bull-statue-scheduled-relocation-stock-exchange-2019-11-1028673614

[h] https://moneymorning.com/2018/02/06/the-10-largest-single-day-losses-for-the-dow-ever/

[i] https://www.sapling.com/784894/average-stock-market-rate-return

[j] https://moneyweek.com/prices-news-charts/dow-jones/

[k] https://moneyweek.com/prices-news-charts/dow-jones/

[l] https://www.mybudget360.com/

[m] https://www.thebalance.com/definition-of-middle-class-income-4126870

[n] https://www.thebalance.com/definition-of-middle-class-income-4126870

[o] https://www.thebalancecareers.com/average-salary-information-for-us-workers-2060808

[p] https://www.census.gov

[q] https://www.census.gov

[r] https://www.marketingcharts.com/

[s] https://www.investopedia.com/terms/m/marketindex.asp

[t] https://www.irs.gov/credits-deductions/individuals/earned-income-tax-credit/earned-income

[u] https://www.goalinvestor.com/

[v] https://www.robinhood.com/

[w] https://apps.apple.com/us/app/ynab-you-need-a-budget/id1010865877

[x] https://apps.apple.com/us/app/mint-personal-finance-money/id300238550

[y] https://smartasset.com/retirement/find-a-financial-planner?utm_source=investopedia&utm_medium=cpc&utm_campaign=inv__falc_ros_textlinks&utm_content=13&utm_term=n4883952fe9b34a50bed9ae582ba3bd7b16

^z https://www.wvpolicy.org/

^{aa} https://www.cnbc.com/2019/05/16/students-families-need-support-systems-to-handle-college-debt-crisis.html

^{bb} https://www.marketwatch.com/story/this-makes-it-even-harder-for-people-to-pay-their-student-loans-2017-03-27

^{cc}https://www.forbes.com/sites/zackfriedman/2019/02/25/student-loan-debt-statistics-2019/#53fa4646133f

^{dd} https://studentaid.ed.gov/sa/fafsa

^{ee} https://www.anthonyoneal.com/scholarships

^{ff} https://www2.ed.gov/about/contacts/state/index.html